GROUND TRUTH

atelier jørgensen, architects

brandon **jørgensen**

ORO
Editions
Novato, California

The New California Modern House

Stanley Saitowitz

The modern house first arrived in California with Rudolph Schindler at Kings Road in Los Angeles in 1922. This was followed by homes by Richard Neutra, Gregory Ain, Raphael Soriano, Harwell Hamilton Harris and others. After the war, Mid Century Modernism emerged in Southern California with the Case Study Houses and the new ephemeral architecture it inspired. Rooted in the world of international modernism, especially Mies van der Rohe, and Japanese minimalism, Craig Ellwood, Pierre Koenig, Charles and Ray Eames and others developed a new aesthetic using both natural and industrially produced materials, reflecting postwar technology, sociology, and cultural landscapes. This work had a significant impact on architecture globally and set the tone for work internationally.

It reached Northern California most robustly in the form of Eichler, where tracts of sublime houses merged with their courts and gardens to become popular frameworks for authentic California life, their structures blurring inside and outside, artifice and nature, escaping the traditional picturesque of craftsman bungalows or Tuscan and Tudor tracts. Architects like Donald Olsen, William Wurster, Joseph Esherick, Claude Oakland, Gardner Dailey, Beverley Thorne and others, built a body of rigorous modern houses scattered over the hills of the Bay Area.

All this came to an end with Sea Ranch. Despite the successes of the original buildings and their appropriateness as low-slung barns on the windswept northern coastline, and the innovative ecological dimensions of the project, it was the picturesque nature of weathered sheds that became both its success and failure as it began to be imitated as a ubiquitous style. Architecture has never emerged from images, and here the picture was paramount. This sold to the public like apple pie, and soon killed the tenuous presence that abstract modernism had begun to establish in the north. Some of the practitioners of Northern California Modernism also strayed into the wooden barn world.

Proof of the shortcoming of architecture based on pictures is what Sea Ranch was precursor of. Its prime authors later trail blazed post-modernism, where architecture was relegated to the spectacle of stage set and a new visual picturesque based on history. The damage of this move-

ment is clear when you see how long it has taken architecture in America to recover. Postwar until Post Modernism America had led the field of architecture. Today it is countries that did not suffer the post-modern tangent: Spain, Portugal, Switzerland, Japan, Mexico and others, who lead.
The architectural recovery of the bay area house was spearheaded by early work of Dan Solomon, the remarkable residences of Jim Jennings, and also Anne Fougeron, me, and others, beginning in the late 1970's and continuing into the present.

Brandon's work is part of the next generation of tenuous modern architecture in California. It is the single-family house that is most strongly the focus of this recovery. Most multifamily housing remains lodged in the picturesque material collage genre of pastiche facades, but scattered around the bay are a robust group of practitioners building contemporary modern homes, and the Ground Truth of Brandon is a significant part of this work.

This contemporary modernism revolves around a sense of Realism in accepting each situation as is without idealization or romanticism and dealing with it accordingly. It involves elevating found conditions to produce form. Realism presents subject matter truthfully, without artificiality and avoiding artistic conventions, implausible exotic elements or stylization. Realism is about actuality not artifice, and portrays the underlying magical nature of the rational world. It is the matter of fact exposure of mysterious reality.

Realism's ideal is optimization. As a search for the authentic, realism involves the aesthetic of removal, letting go of the unnecessary. An example is the Tesla Model 3 dashboard. No dials, instruments, buttons, louvers - a single slot for all air handling, and an iPad like screen for all controls and information. A complete reassessment of functionality without sentimentality. Realism eschews romanticism and decoration: patterns, frames, arbitrary details, are replaced by instruments, devices for others to make their own, where taste is absent, and aesthetic not imposed. Neutral tools to liberate others and make their worlds. Key to realism is user interface and user experience. Realist work proceeds from ideas - first why, only then does how enter. In realist architecture bathrooms are about bathroomness (water/cleansing), kitchens about kitchenness (fire storage) like appliances or fixtures - not designs. Realism uses materials directly for their character and quality and reveals their presence and assembly in construction.

Realism's branches are contextualism and regionalism, and the close relationship to climate, geography, and territory, establishing dialogue with the land, sun, wind and water. The inherent qualities of location and geography are mirrored in the architecture through materials that reflect nature and the surrounding environment, and space that is a lens that blurs the distinction between found and made, nature and artifact. The aim is to enable the pleasures of occasion, the enjoyment of gathering, the tranquility of solitude, through the intensification and sanctification of everyday life.

The most striking sensibility Brandon brings to the houses is via their materiality, their machined earthiness, the way they echo the ground, the textures of the trees and hills, and how they reflect the sky.

At the Oak Knoll Residence the huge plane of roof is lifted like a piece of floating ground from the valley floor. It hovers over the habitable space, buttressed by extrusions of rock and piles of timber. This gliding plane both extends and shelters, mirroring the flat topography, creating a new hollow stratum within for the joy of occupation.

The same roof as raised ground plane shelters the Jørgensen Residence, but here in a wooded setting that it reflects with its timber lining. The house begins as a battered earth plinth, a new elevated ground supporting a cave-like interior, sheltered and cool like a forest which the roof hangs over to extend into the surrounding dense vegetation. Where Oak Knoll is a valley floor house, Jørgensen is a forest retreat.

The taught box of Mount Veeder Outpost is a single carved object where wall and roof merge in continuous folds that create the exterior and shape the interior. A giant corner of glass dissolves the folded box into the landscape. The striped siding mirrors the bark of surrounding tall pines which the object is lodged in. Trailside Winery, like the stakes on which vines learn to grow, is structure as infrastructure, an ephemeral cathedral of grape stakes in which to make wine. Ink Grade Winery explores the floating plane of roof to its fullest, a hovering hill, suspended cloudlike over the winemaking apparatus it protects, sanctifying winemaking in an air and light filled barn.

Cliffhanger Cabin is a relative of Mount Veeder Outpost, here a sculpted rather than folded object, treelike and counter curved to dodge trees, twisted to throw off snow. The complex double arc interlocking forms complement and counter the pine forest and snow. Filtered Lanai is pure Hawaii where a dappled porch is all the shelter needed in its climate. This house blurs any difference between inside and out in a way that defies entering or leaving.

Each of the projects Brandon Jørgensen presents in Ground Truth brings to focus its unique site and situation becoming a lens that amplifies the world it inhabits, defining the nature of the New California Modern House.

405

Harris Wine Library

Napa, California 2017

HALL
MEZCAL
Nahuales.
special edition

MEZCAL

2015
2016
2016

Jørgensen Residence

Napa Valley, California 2017

Mount Veeder Outpost

Napa Valley, California 2020

BOCUSE
ROBUCHON

PIMM'S

Trailside Winery

Napa Valley, California 2021

Ink Grade Winery

Saint Helena, California 2022

Cliffhanger Cabin

Alpine Meadows, California 2022

Filtered Lanai

Waimea, Hawaii 2022

65-1226

65-1226

Ground Truth

Ground Truth

Brandon Jørgensen

In 1989, I graduated high school early to escape the hardship I called life at that time. I was flunking out of every class, I was frustrated, and did not have the wherewithal to go off to college. So, I did what any sane 18-year-old would do, I joined the army. The army was, in my opinion, the only way I could take charge of my future. I had no idea about the world of architecture, and only wanted to shake loose what had been my life to that point.

My four years in the 10th Mountain Division taught me discipline, gave me confidence in myself, and made me decide that I wanted to leave the world in a better place than I had found it. My first indication that architecture was something other than the local public library or the McDonalds down the street, existing only to house our needs, came after I finished the army. It was a spring day in 1993 in California and I saw the world completely different after four long years of ordered chaos, extremes, and total adventure.

There's a picture somewhere of me with my bleached blonde hair, ray bans, sitting by the pool toasting the world with a Coors light, wearing boardshorts and a tank top, having never stepped foot on a surfboard, a true kook.

There is no way in hell you can understand my process for design and or my buildings unless you understand that 22-year-old sitting there pretending to be someone cool. That pool was in the backyard of what most Americans grew up around – a tract house!

...they were not beautiful or cool.

Architecture and the discovery of 'it' was the path I saw forward. In the world of architecture now, I just try to hide out and do what I think is the good stuff. So, what, I came up in a hard world, full of generalities, pragmatics, and darkness. There was no time for any other world, other than to think of one as some far-off spectrum of the world that I didn't necessarily want to be a part of. So, in this world of Architecture, flying off to meet with a celebrity, or sitting down at a table with a billionaire, is both foreign and very comfortable at the same time.

This world sometimes feels like the time you meet that beautiful person who you know outclasses you on every level, but for one reason or another they are attracted to you and want to know you. You marry that person!

Outclassed, outgunned, and intimidated, but you want all of it and you want to know it. So, like any confident and driven person you reach deep down and go for what you want. This world is full of buildings that are often ineffable pieces of sculpture, new and or a thousand years old, or some flaccid superficial big box retail store. All of this is inconceivable if your eyes haven't been open to where you have seen it, where you have felt it. I mean, most of my life was spent in some mediocre suburban environment, where everything around you has been produced by a machine that only wants you to buy and possess more things.

For the most part, now having been in this profession for the 30 something years I have, I still think about how I existed without seeing, feeling, or thinking about the built environment around me. Sure, I thought about buildings in the context of construction, I always liked how beautiful a new house was when it was under construction. I liked bigger projects even more, like a freeway overpass or a bridge under construction, to this day, I spend a lot of time on construction sites to see and feel how it is all coming together. I know more about construction than most of my peers to this day because of it.

This oblivious nature in which my senses missed most of what architecture had to offer has shaped me differently. Sure, I have read or seen movies where there were great buildings and icons, but none of them drew me to them. Only later in my life have I slowly visited them and understood their power on humanity. Like that first kiss we all had, where we felt like the world revolved around a single moment of ecstasy. That kiss though, isn't a kiss until you have it! That's how architecture is, until that desire is there, it is invisible. Without getting too potent and sticking to the pragmatics, the term "ground truth" for me was first introduced when I was in the Army. Before a mission or operation, we would be briefed by the intelligence team about the topography, weather, and other pertinent information. No matter what, none of what we were told was the actual situation on the ground when my team arrived. Someone would quip, "ground truth" and it was understood universally. Over the years in this profession of design and building. A visceral feeling was always there when I was drawing a detail, or trying to make sure each corner of a building's juncture was thought out, to the point where I started to resent the "verify in field" comment, which to me was a sloppy way of suggesting that we didn't have time for this until later.

Before we understand my relation to the term, ground truth, with regards to architecture, we must first understand its root (etymology). Not all of you immediately jump to the OED (Oxford English Dictionary) and frankly, it's a little snooty that I am starting there, but I am a nerd who likes my facts and stories. Hell, maybe I use the damn thing as a crutch like most, however, I suggest going out and finding a copy to have some fun, in a nerdy way of course.

The OED has several definitions for the term "ground truth." The first being related to Henry Ellison's poem "The Siberian Exile's Tale," (a beautiful poem) where it is believed or inferred that Mr. Ellison uses "groundtruth" in his poem, published in 1833, to express a "fundamental truth." An all-knowing truth covering all bases of human existence. This is my interpretation though, some of you may disagree.

The second definition has to do more with science when making maps, where measuring the ground through remote sensing such as through aerial or satellite imagery to verify or calibrate an understanding of topography, versus by direct measurement at the ground level which is obtaining factual data from being on the ground or obtaining the "ground truth." Data being collected or obtained at a distance rather than by measurements made on location. Without getting into how the two, go hand in hand, you should know that I believe again, this is a form of the scientific method where assumptions are made and then they are accurately measured when a person is on the ground. In most instances of reading through the sources defining the term in the OED, I and many others all begin to realize that a very clear line points to the term being a lexicon within military reconnaissance—throughout history, the question of "what is happening on the ground?" and where "on the ground" refers to a point over the line of sight or a distant location where the action is happening.

The third definition relates to machine learning, where information is obtained by direct observation of a real system, as opposed to a model or simulation. You know, that set of data that is considered to be accurate (construction documents for example) and reliable, and is used to calibrate a model, algorithm, procedure, etc. Without getting into the depths of this science, of AI, you all can read a great book, The Singularity is Near by Ray Kurzweil. A very thoughtful and in-depth book full of pragmatic information regarding technology and our human interaction with it. This is for another time though.

Ground truth in my opinion, has never been the absolute or right answer with regards to architecture. There is no verification in the field. In my world of architecture or the practice of building, where Ken Frampton's "tectonics" (Studies in Tectonic Culture: The Poetics of Construction in the Nineteenth and Twentieth Century Architecture, Penguin Random House, 2001) are concerned, getting one's hands dirty in order to resolve a connection or transition in a building, no matter what size, is the Ground Truth. Our office jargon of ground truth refers to the actual situation of construction and building as opposed to design and documentation or the assumptive situation.

Tactility is a key element with regards to the way we design at Atelier Jørgensen. Our office is based on combining all our resources. Drawing by hand, making mock-ups, and building models is an integral part of our process. In the field during construction this iterative approach continues where the hand stays connected to our design. We are not afraid to pick up a nail gun or skill saw to show our craftsman what we are thinking. This approach is what we have referred to as our Ground Truth—if you understand your methods and means, it will allow you to always be creative, edit, and refine with authority. However, this does not mean that one solution can be applied universally or that that process is the absolute right answer; in fact, the ground truth becomes a discovery or journey.

Operations + Instruments

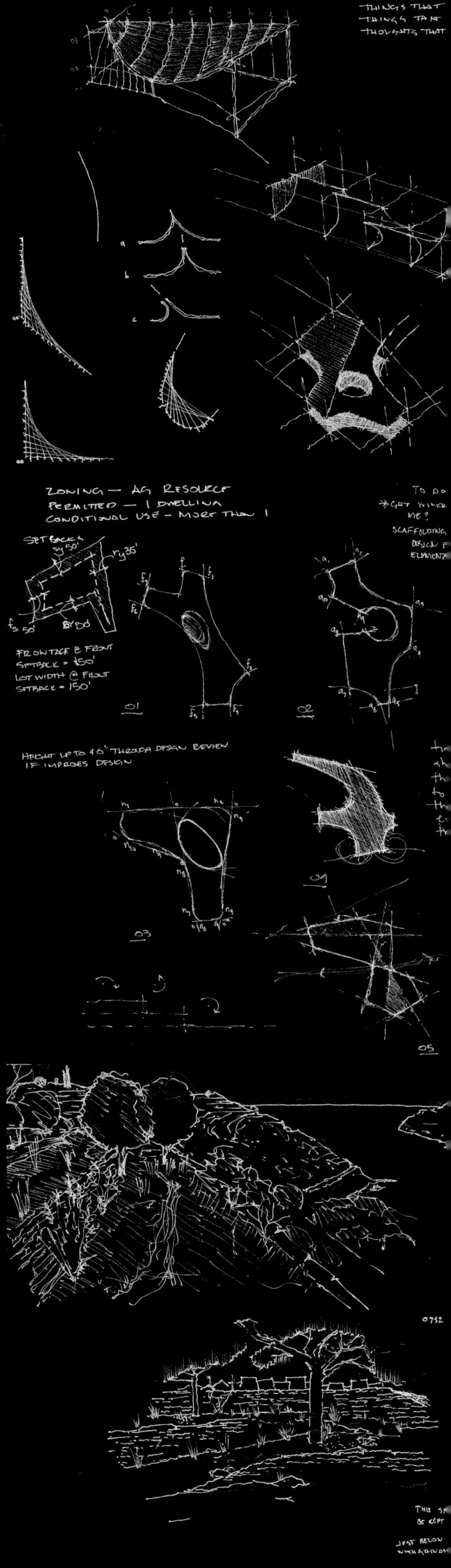
ZONING — AG RESOURCE
PERMITTED — 1 DWELLING
CONDITIONAL USE — MORE THAN 1
SETBACKS
FRONTAGE @ FRONT
SETBACK = 150'
LOT WIDTH @ FRONT
SETBACK = 150'
01
02
TO DO
SCAFFOLDING
HEIGHT UP TO 40' THROUGH DESIGN REVIEW
IF IMPROVES DESIGN
03
04
05

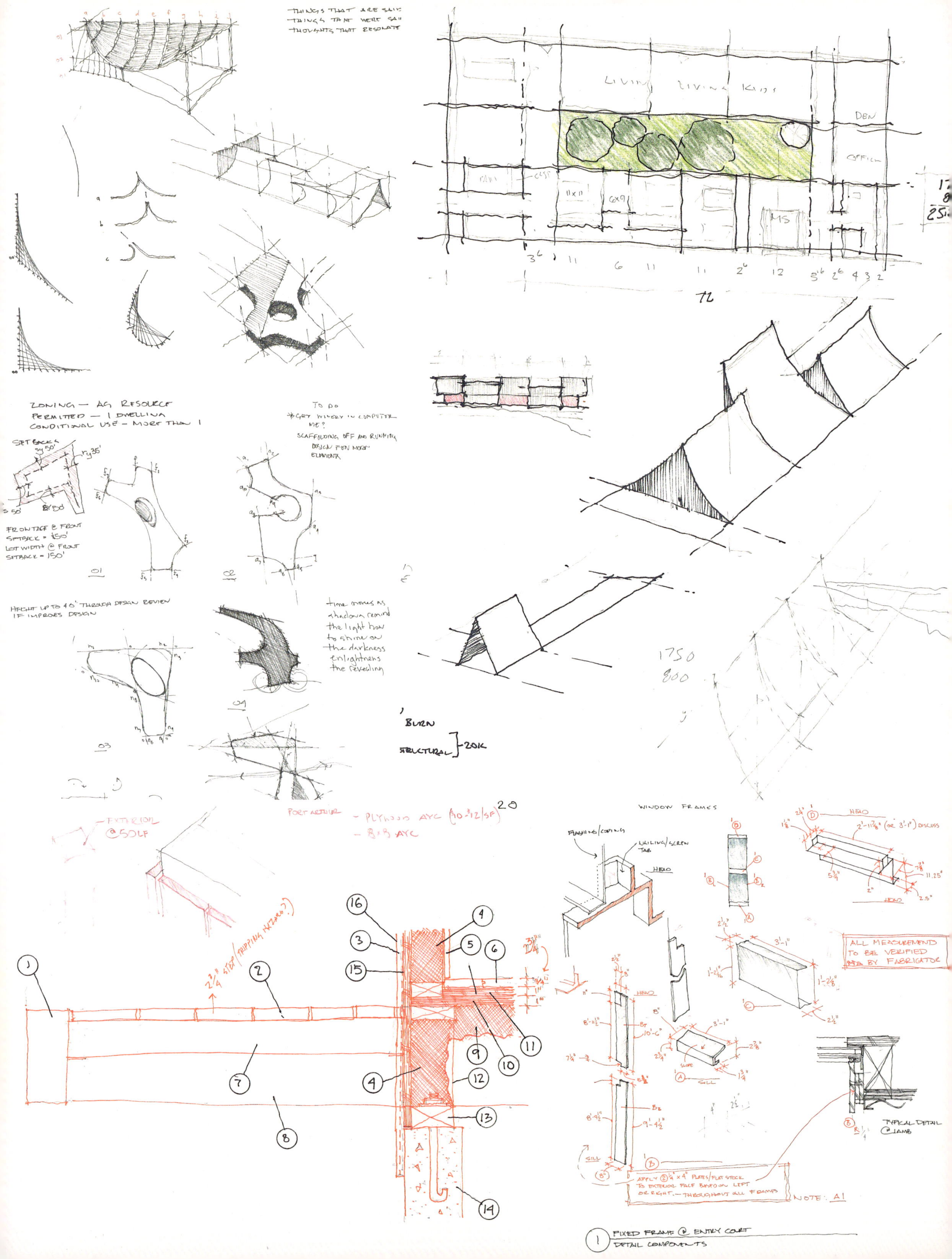

THINGS THAT ARE SAID
THINGS THAT WERE SAID
THOUGHTS THAT RESONATE
DEN
OFFICE
MS
72
ZONING — AG RESOURCE
PERMITTED — 1 DWELLING
CONDITIONAL USE — MORE THAN 1
TO DO
GET WINERY IN COMPUTER
ME?
SCAFFOLDING OFF AND RUNNING
DESIGN FOR MORE ELEMENTS
SETBACK
FRONTAGE @ FRONT SETBACK = 150'
LOT WIDTH @ FRONT SETBACK = 150'
01
02
HEIGHT UP TO 40' THROUGH DESIGN REVIEW IF IMPROVES DESIGN
time moves as shadows remind the light how to shine on the darkness enlightens the revealing
03
04
1750
800
BURN
STRUCTURAL
20K
EXTERIOR @ 50LF
PORT ARTHUR
— PLYWOOD AYC (10-12/SF)
— B+B AYC
20
2 3/4" STEP (TRIPPING HAZARD?)
WINDOW FRAMES
FLASHING/COPING
NAILING/SCREEN TAB
HEAD
SILL
ALL MEASUREMENTS TO BE VERIFIED BY FABRICATOR
TYPICAL DETAIL @ JAMB
APPLY 2 1/4 x 4" PLATES/FLAT STOCK TO EXTERIOR FACE BASED ON LEFT OR RIGHT — THROUGHOUT ALL FRAMES
NOTE: A1
FIXED FRAME @ ENTRY COURT
DETAIL COMPONENTS

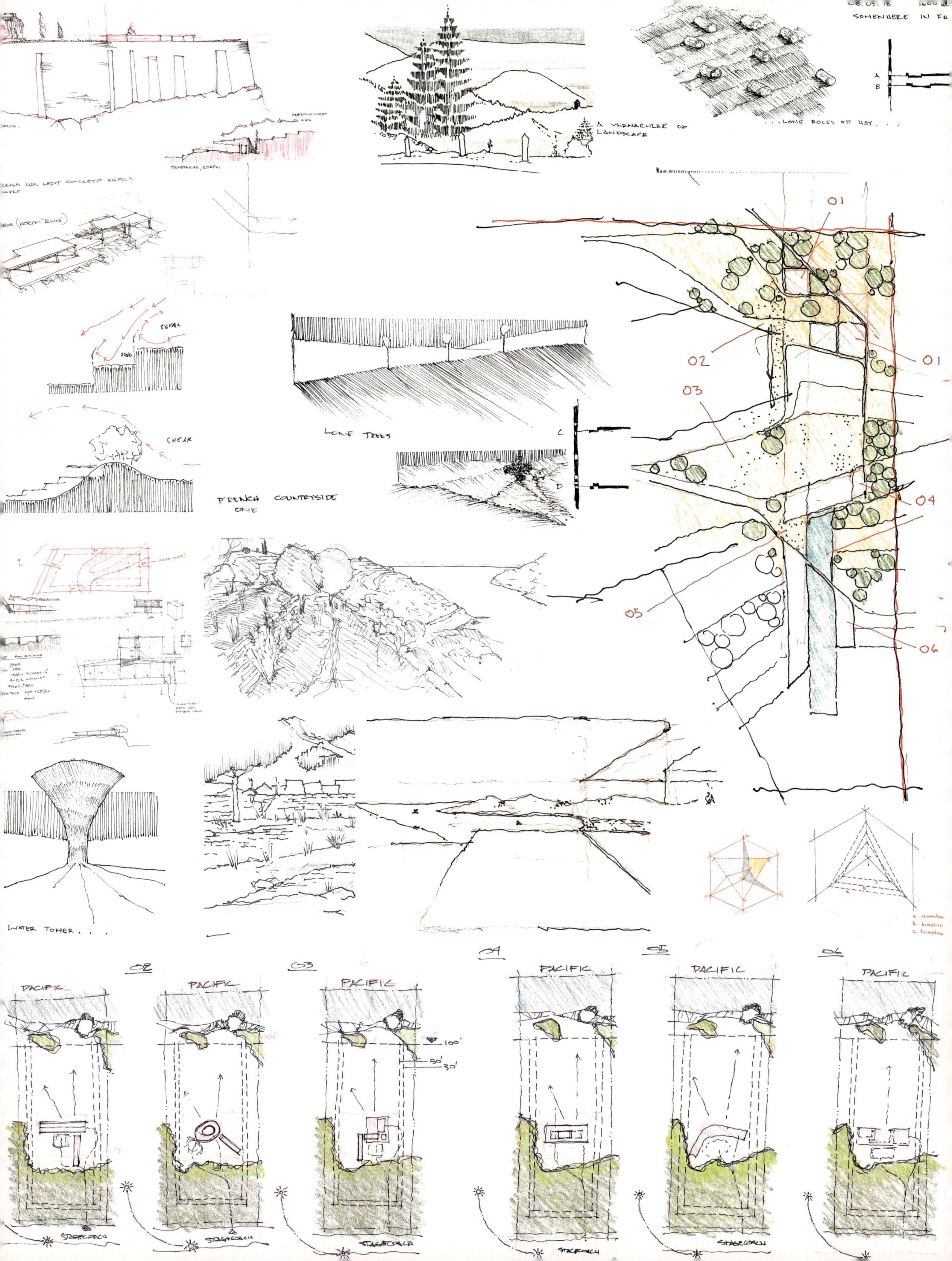
A VERNACULAR OF LANDSCAPE
. . . LONE ROLES OF HAY . . .
SHEAR
LONE TREES
FRENCH COUNTRYSIDE ONE
01
02
03
04
05
06
WATER TOWER . . .
PACIFIC
100'
50'
30'
STAGECOACH

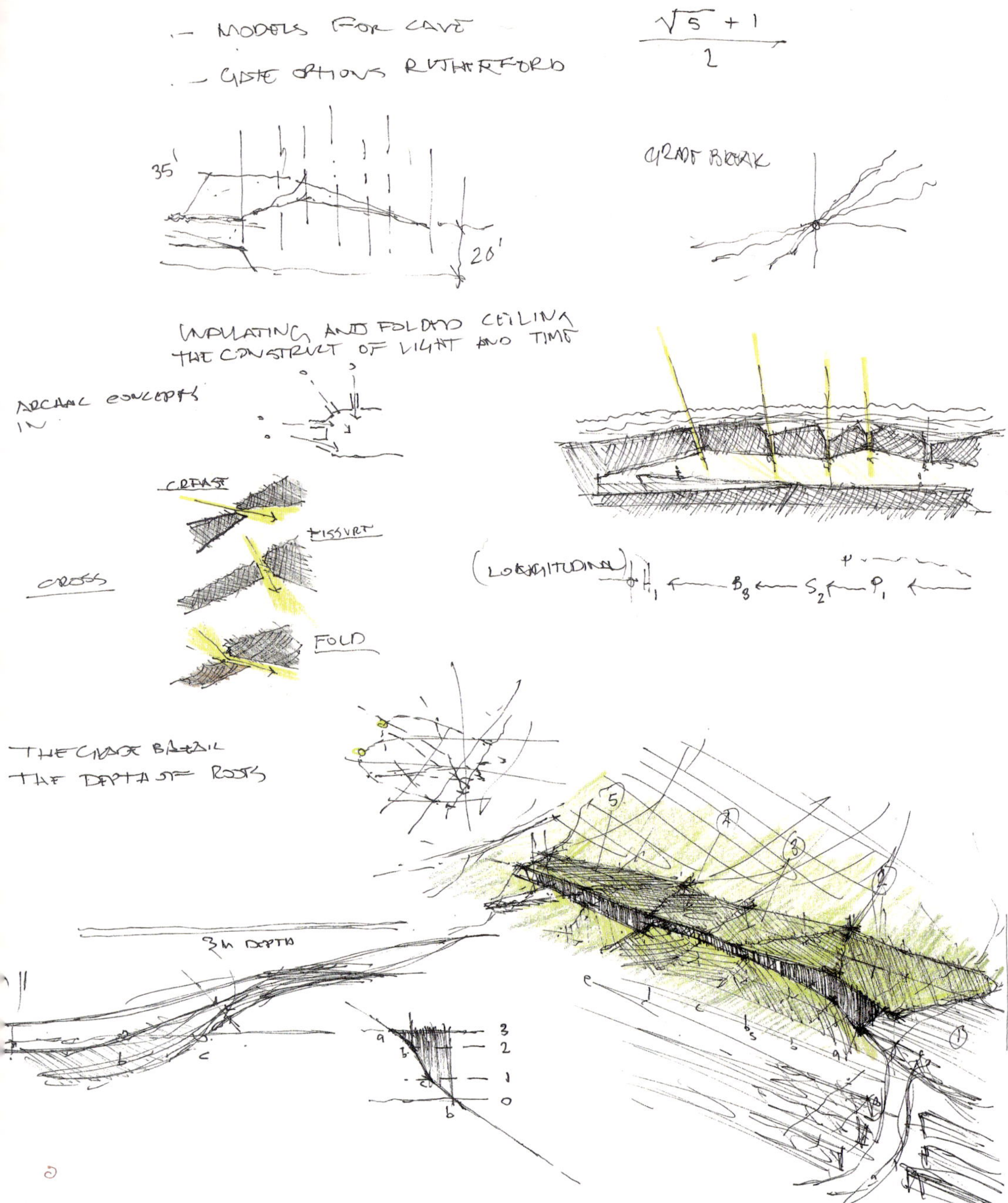

– MODELS FOR CAVE
– GATE OPTIONS RUTHERFORD
$\frac{\sqrt{5}+1}{2}$
35'
20'
GRADE BREAK
UNDULATING AND FOLDED CEILING
THE CONSTRUCT OF LIGHT AND TIME
ARCHAIC CONCEPTS IN
CREASE
FISSURE
CROSS
FOLD
(LONGITUDINAL)
THE GRADE BREAK
THE DEPTH OF ROOTS
3M DEPTH

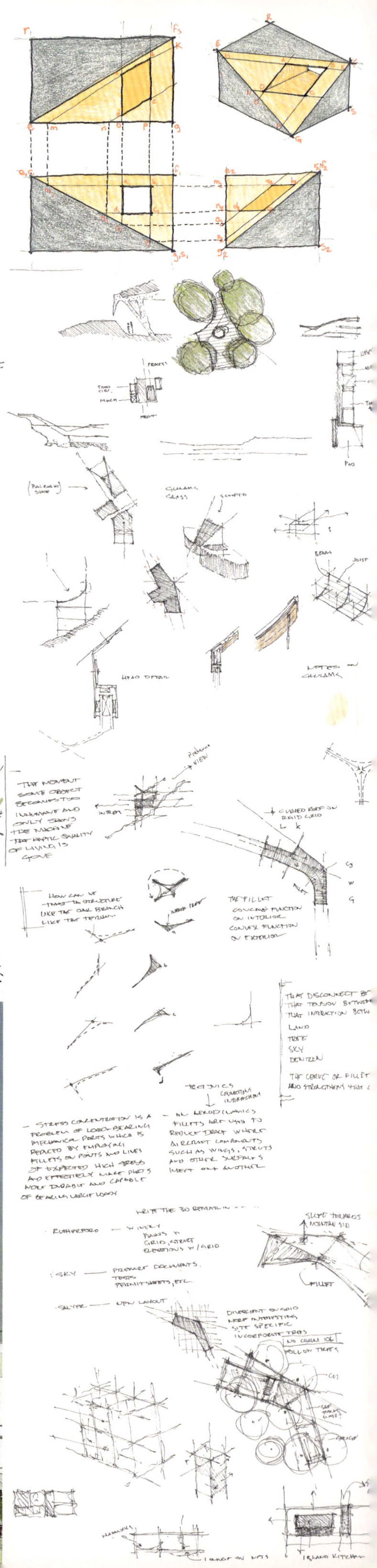

THE MOMENT SOME OBJECT BECOMES TOO ILLUMINATED AND ONLY SHOWS THE MACHINE THE HAPTIC QUALITY OF LIVING IS GONE
HOW CAN WE THE STRUCTURE LIKE THE OAK BRANCH LIKE THE TERRAIN
THE FILLET CONCAVE FUNCTION ON INTERIOR CONVEX FUNCTION ON EXTERIOR
THAT DISCONNECT BT
THAT TENSION BETWEEN
THAT INTERACTION BETW
LAND
TREE
SKY
DENIZEN
– STRESS CONCENTRATION IS A PROBLEM OF LOAD BEARING MECHANICAL PARTS WHICH IS REDUCED BY EMPLOYING FILLETS ON POINTS AND LINES OF EXPECTED HIGH STRESS AND EFFECTIVELY MAKE PARTS MORE DURABLE AND CAPABLE OF BEARING LARGE LOADS
– IN AERODYNAMICS FILLETS ARE USED TO REDUCE DRAG WHERE AIRCRAFT COMPONENTS SUCH AS WINGS, STRUTS AND OTHER SURFACES MEET ONE ANOTHER
RUTHERFORD
SKY
FILLET

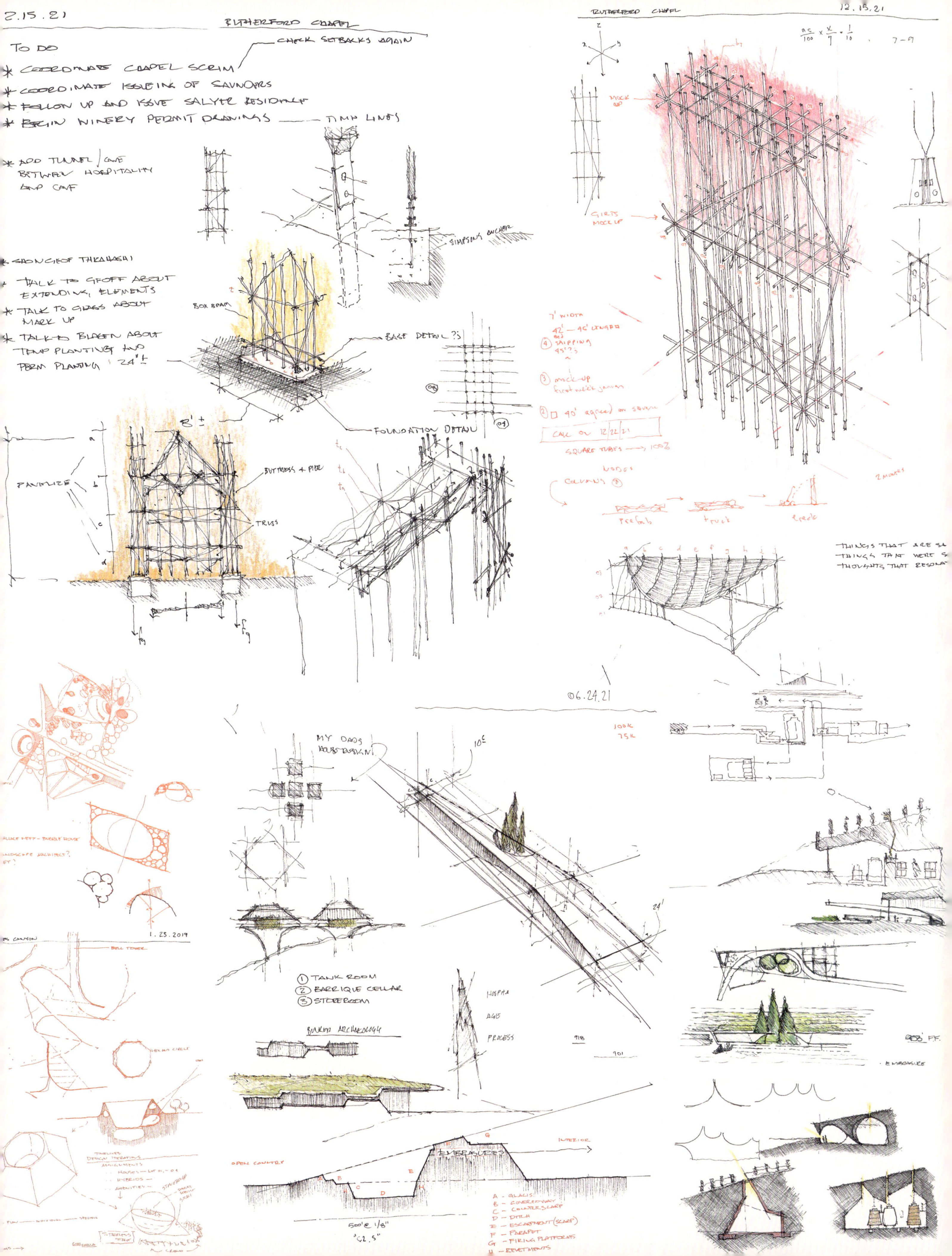

2.15.21
RUTHERFORD CHAPEL
TO DO
CHECK SETBACKS AGAIN
* COORDINATE CHAPEL SCRIM
* COORDINATE ISSUING OF SAVNOPRS
* FOLLOW UP AND ISSUE SALYER RESIDENCE
* BEGIN WINERY PERMIT DRAWINGS
TIMP LINES
* ADD TUNNEL / CAVE BETWEEN HOSPITALITY AND CAVE
SIMPSON ANCHOR
TALK TO GEOFF ABOUT EXTENDING ELEMENTS
* TALK TO GLASS ABOUT MARK UP
* TALK TO BLAKEN ABOUT TEMP PLANTING AND PERM PLANTING 24"±
BOX BEAM
BASE DETAIL ?s
FOUNDATION DETAIL
8'±
BUTTRESS + PIER
TRUSS
PANELIZE
RUTHERFORD CHAPEL
12.15.21
MOCK UP
GIRTS MOCK UP
7' WIDTH
42' - 45' LENGTH
SHIPPING
mock-up first week januar
CALL ON 12/22/21
SQUARE TUBES 100%
COLUMNS
prefab
truck
crane
2 MOVERS
THINGS THAT ARE S
THINGS THAT WERE S
THOUGHTS THAT RESONA
06.24.21
100K
75K
MY DADS
10°
24'
1. 23. 2019
BELL TOWER
① TANK ROOM
② BARRIQUE CELLAR
③ STOREROOM
HOSPITA
AGE
PROCESS
918
901
EMBRASURE
OPEN COUNTRY
INTERIOR
EMBRASURES
A - GLACIS
B - COVEREDWAY
C - COUNTERSCARP
D - DITCH
E - ESCARPMENT (SCARP)
F - PARAPET
G - FIRING PLATFORMS
H - REVETMENTS
500'@ 1/8"
"C2.5"

12.07.98
07.12.98
ROYAL ACADEMY
CRITICAL MASS

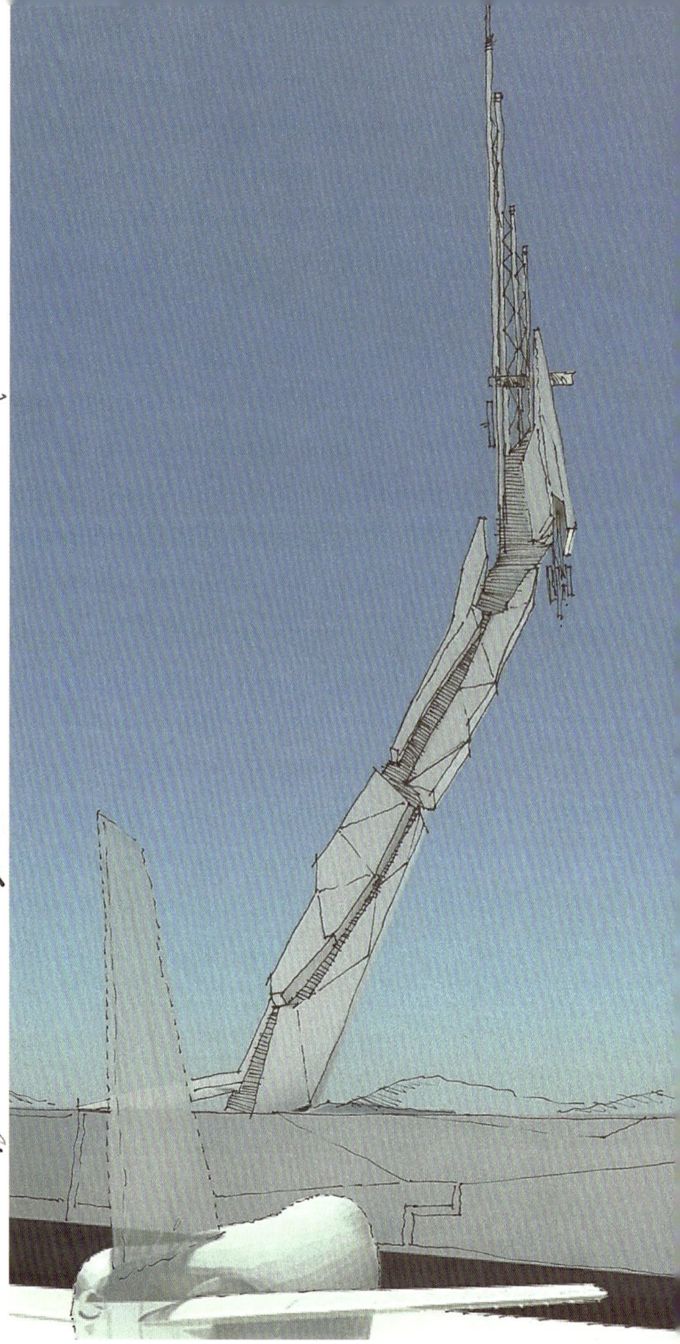

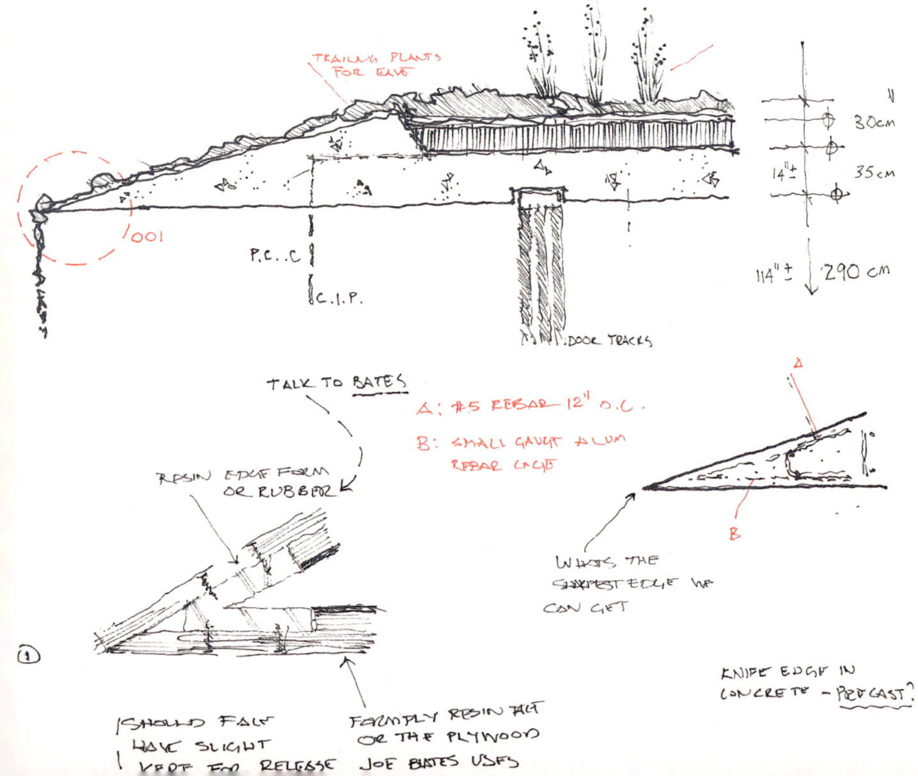
TRAILING PLANTS FOR EAVE
30cm
14"±
35cm
001
P.C.C
C.I.P.
114"±
290 cm
DOOR TRACKS
TALK TO BATES
A: #5 REBAR 12" O.C.
B: SMALL GAUGE ALUM REBAR CAGE
RESIN EDGE FORM OR RUBBER
B
WHATS THE SHARPEST EDGE WE CAN GET
KNIFE EDGE IN CONCRETE - PRECAST?
SHOULD FACE HAVE SLIGHT KERF FOR RELEASE
FORMPLY RESIN TACT OR THE PLYWOOD JOE BATES USES

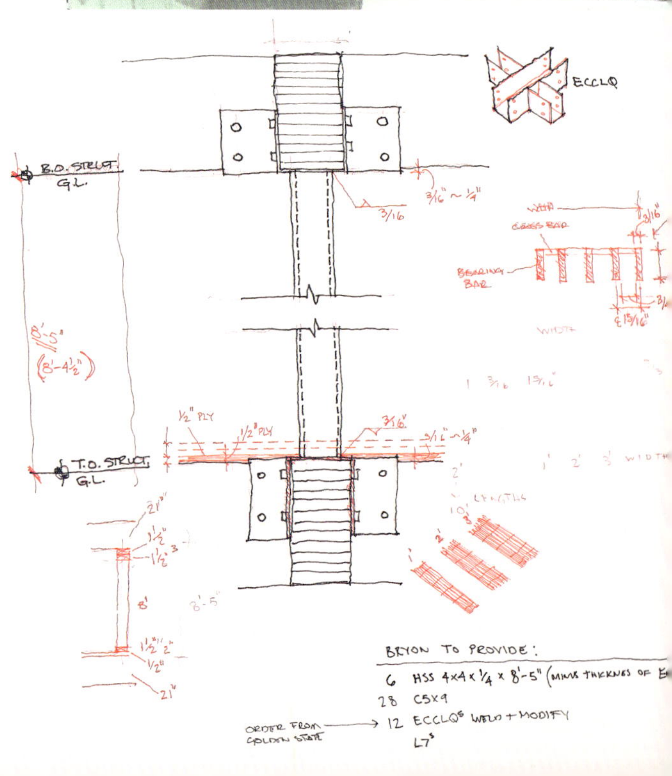
ECCLQ
B.O. STRUCT. G.L.
T.O. STRUCT. G.L.
8'-5"
(8'-4½")
BRYON TO PROVIDE:
6 HSS 4x4x¼ x 8'-5"
28 C5x9
12 ECCLQ6 WELD + MODIFY
L7
ORDER FROM GOLDEN STATE

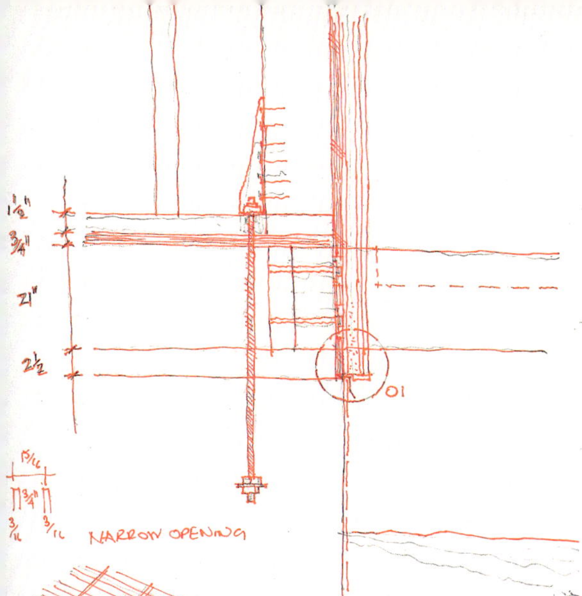

	B	F
CORNER 2	1@ 5/8" 24"	1 @ 5/8" 24"
2.3	2@ 5/8 x 24"	2@ 5/8" x 24"
2.6	2@ 5/8 x 24"	2@ 5/8" x 24"
3	1@ 1" x 48" + 1@ 5/8" x 24"	2@ 5/8" x 24"
4	2@ 5/8" x 24"	1@ 1" x 48" + 1@ 5/8" x 24"
4.5	2@ 5/8" x 24"	2@ 5/8" x 24"
5 CORNER	1@ 5/8" x 24"	1@ 1" x 48" + 1@ 5/8" x 24"
6		

22 @ 5/8" x 24"
7 @ 1" x 48"

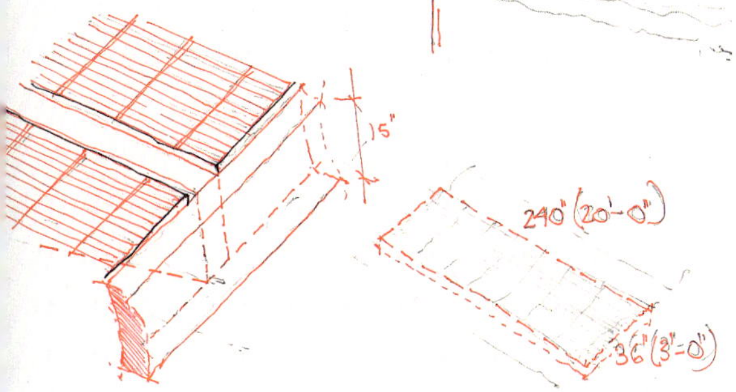

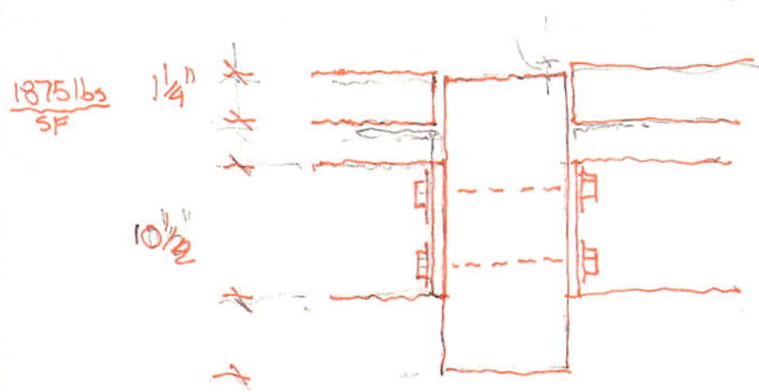

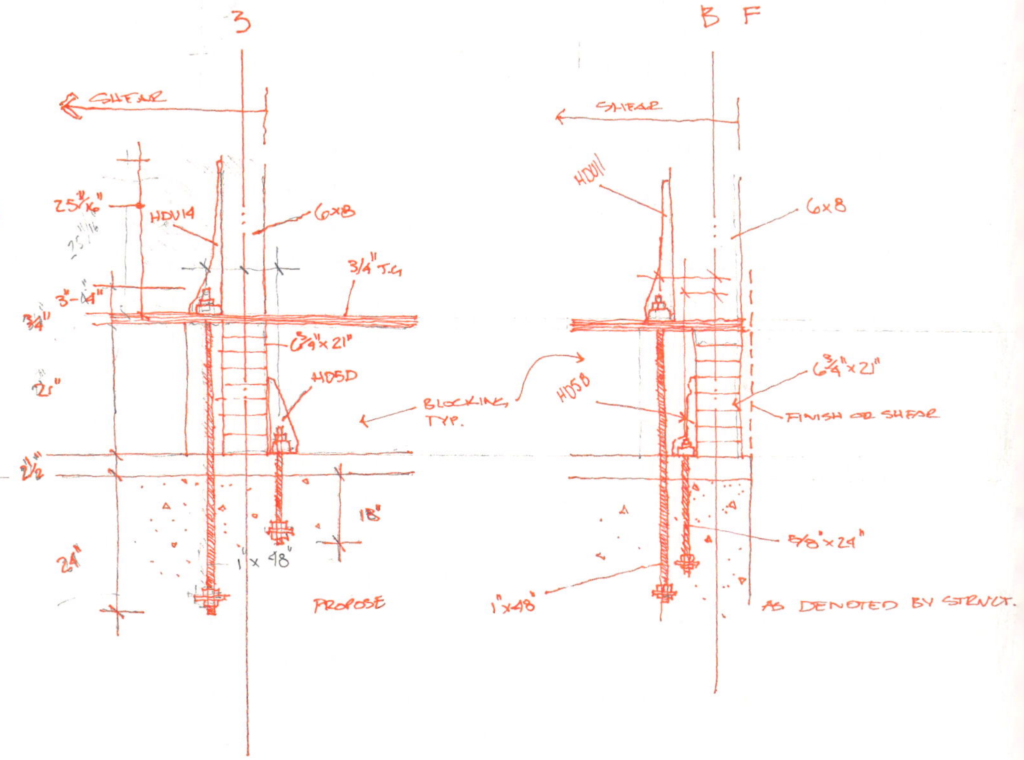

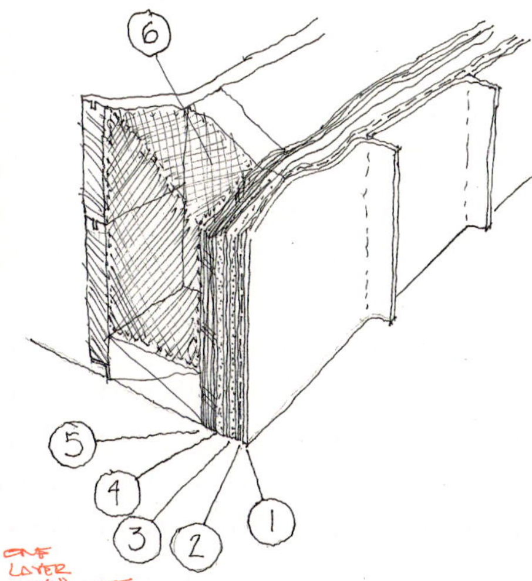

ONE LAYER 5/8" NOT TWO

1. STEEL PLATE W/ BREAK
2. VAPOR BARRIER
3/4. ONE LAYER 5/8" GYP.
5. 1/2" PLY SHEAR
6. RIGID INSULATION

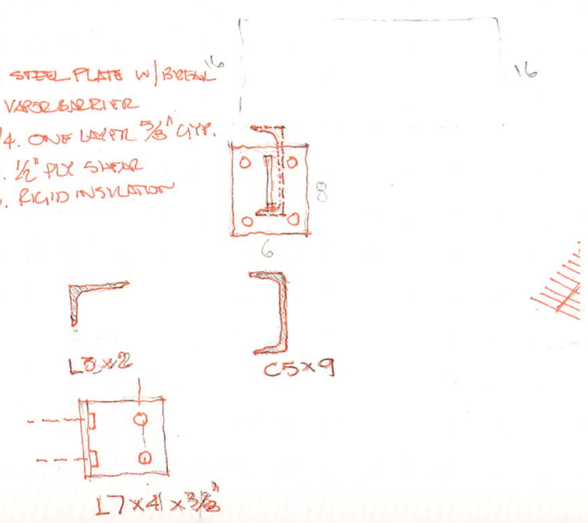

1. STONE OR CERAMIC TILE
2. WATERPROOFING OVER BACKER BOARD
3. SPRAY FOAM INSULATION
4. 1/2" SHEAR PLYWOOD
5. TYPE 'X' 5/8" BOARD
6. VAPOR BARRIER
7. 1/4" REFLECTIVE BOARD
8. STEEL PLATES

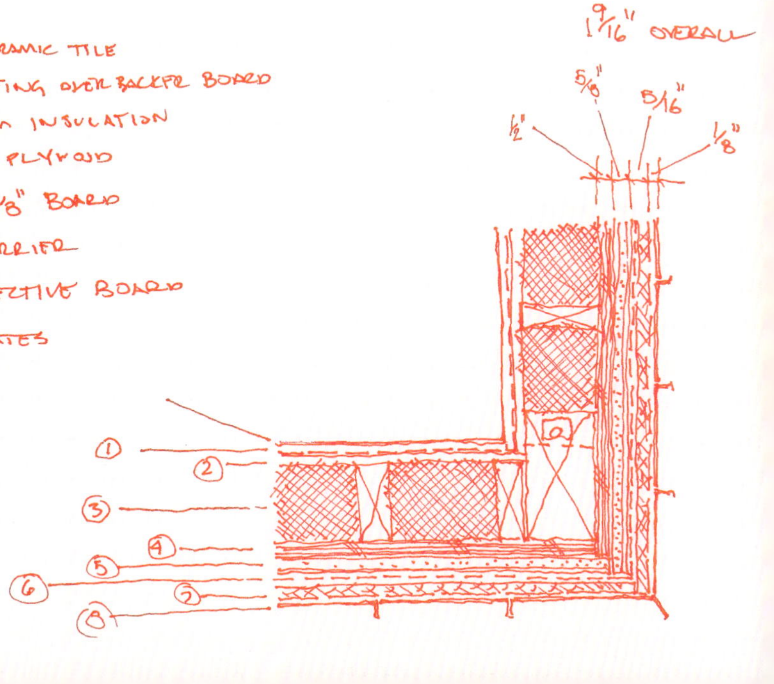

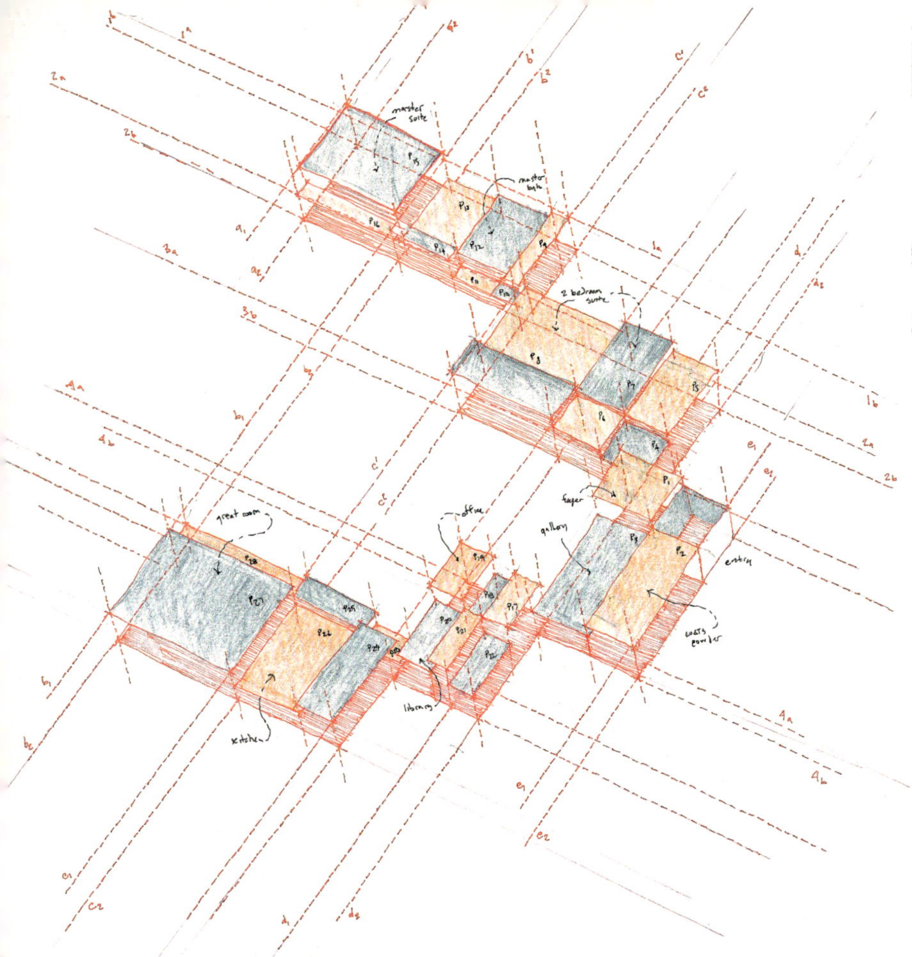
master suite
master bath
2 bedroom suite
great room
office
gallery
foyer
entry
kitchen
library

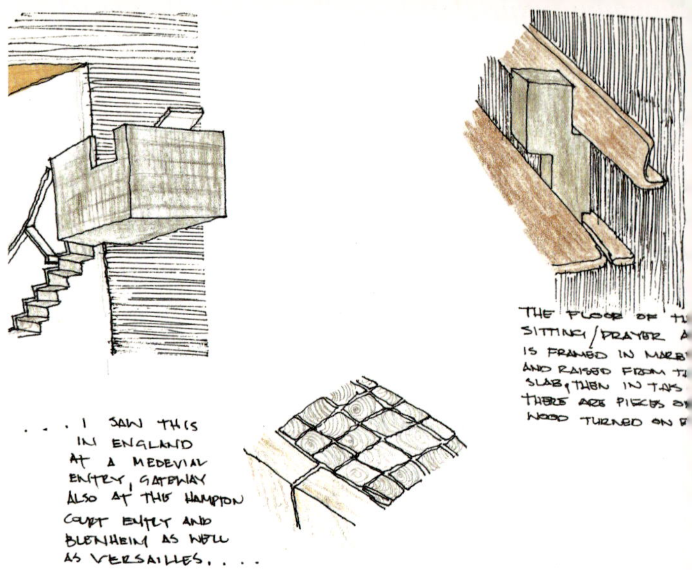
. . . I SAW THIS IN ENGLAND AT A MEDEVIAL ENTRY, GATEWAY ALSO AT THE HAMPTON COURT ENTRY AND BLENHEIM AS WELL AS VERSAILLES. . . .
THE FLOOR OF TH
SITTING/PRAYER A
IS FRAMED IN MARB
AND RAISED FROM TH
SLAB, THEN IN THIS
THERE ARE PIECES O
WOOD TURNED ON E

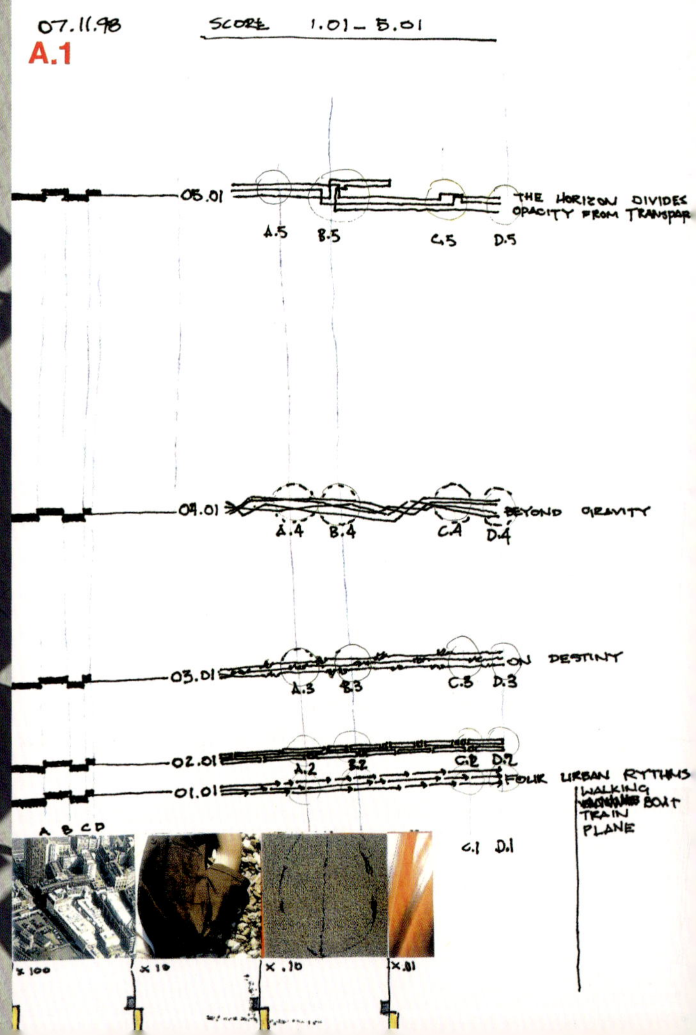
07.11.98
SCORE 1.01 – 5.01
05.01
THE HORIZON DIVIDES OPACITY FROM TRANSPAR
A.5 B.5 C.5 D.5
04.01
BEYOND GRAVITY
A.4 B.4 C.4 D.4
03.01
ON DESTINY
A.3 B.3 C.3 D.3
02.01
A.2 B.2 C.2 D.2
01.01
FOUR URBAN RYTHMS
WALKING
BOAT
TRAIN
PLANE
A B C D
C.1 D.1
X 100
X 10
X .10
X .01

A.1

20 MINS. AT VILLA LA ROCHE
CORBUSIER
CORBS FORM
25071
FONDATION LE CORBUSIER
10 SQUARE DU DOCTEUR BLANCHE 75016 PARIS
... HOW LIGHT MOVES ...
C.3
SALVO
S.1
HOLLISTIC
H.1
TORQUE
T.1
FORMAL
F.1
RITUAL
R.1
MAJOR NODES BECOME FORMAL
RESTRICT A VIEW PERTAINING TO
THE FORMAL STRUCTURE
OF THE CITY
X1.200
X.037
X.00
her eyes to see
the future
The festival
the path
tactical insertion
COUNTERBALANCE
The conscience
the combination
The ancient
the eye
the culture
the threshold
the complexity
no modern
the prosthetic
the temples
the environmental
the hand
The late
D.4
FROM SOUTH
10:31
FROM NORTH
10:51
FROM EAST
10:39
SUMMER SOLSTICE 06.21.99
8.4.19
ALHAMBRA, GRANADA
FOR AS SLOPPY, MISPROPORTIONED, AND RUINOUS GENERALIFE IS, THERE IS SO MUCH TO LEARN FROM THIS PLACE
LOOS, MIES, CORBU, WRIGHT, KHAN, ETC... BARRAGAN.. HAVE LEARNED FROM HERE AND HAVE EVEN COME
PASEO DE LAS TORRES GARDENS
GARDEN PROCES...
GARDEN
THIS IS A VALVE MADE OF CERAMIC TO CONTROL WATER MOVING FROM ONE GARDEN TO ANOTHER
ROYAL COURT
COMMERCE
BUREAUCRACY
ALHAMBRA PALACE
HEDGES SURROUNDING GARDENS
OFFICERS QUARTER - ALHAMBRA
STREET
SOLDIERS BARRACKS
NATURAL POOL
THAT ART TRUN
GENERALIFE

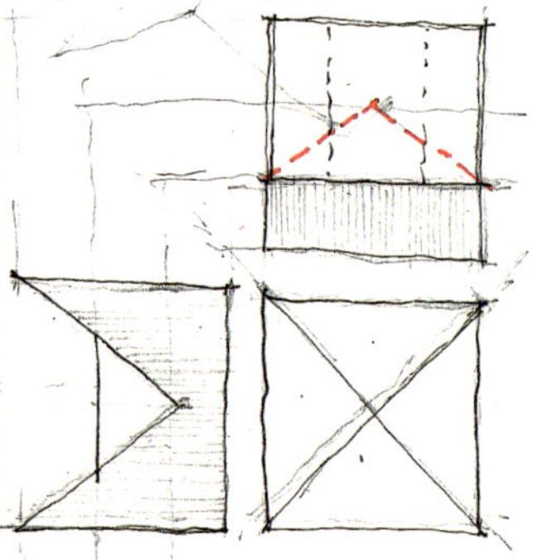

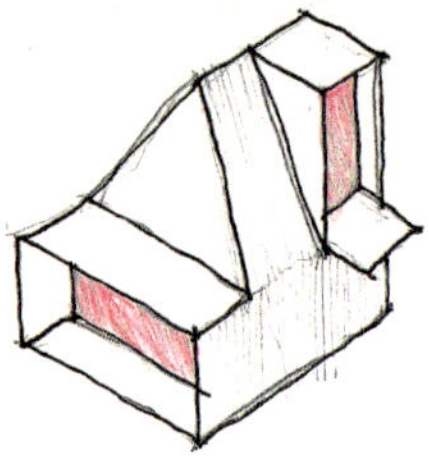

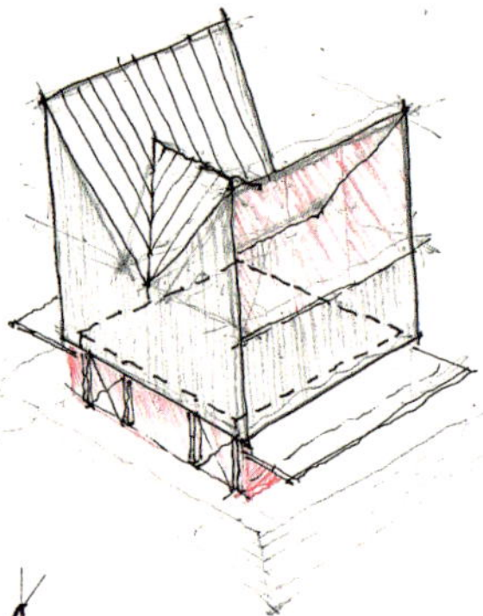

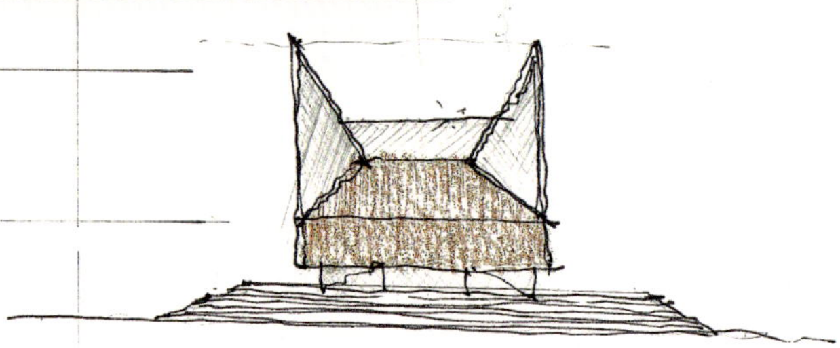

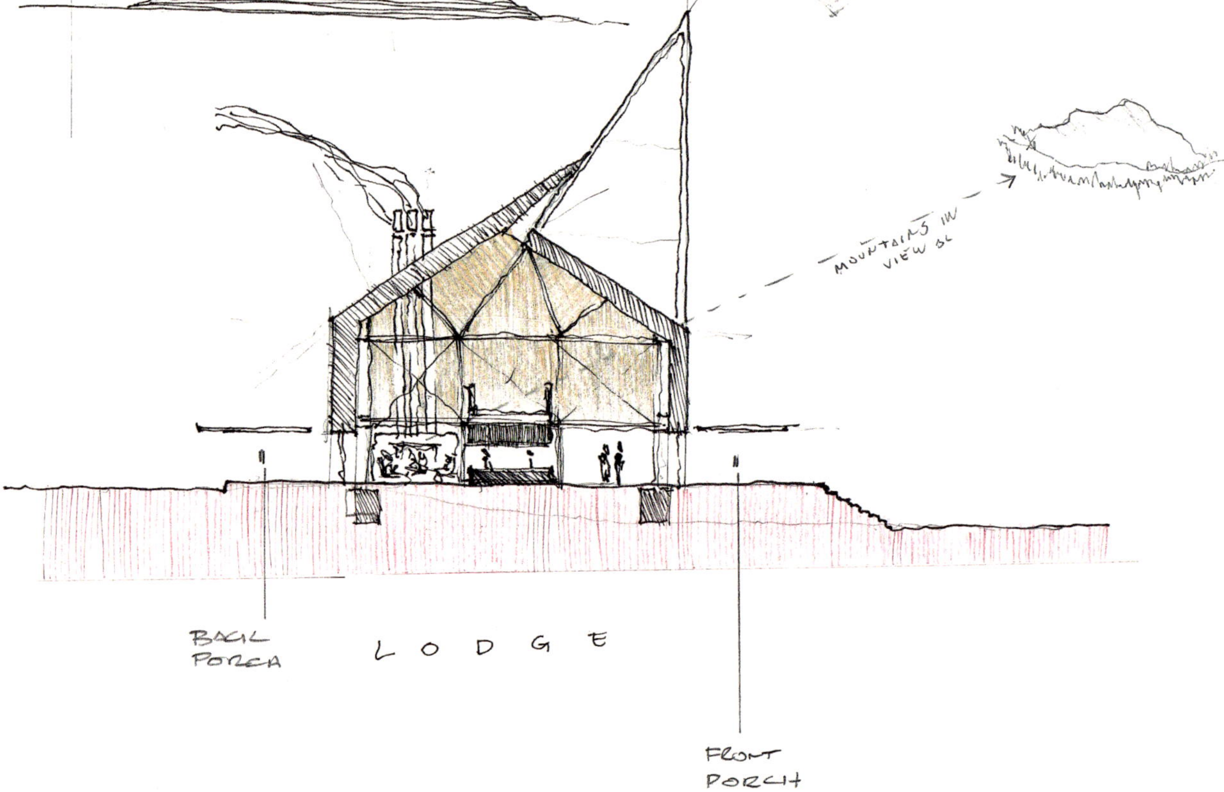
MOUNTAINS IN VIEW
BACK PORCH
LODGE
FRONT PORCH

STABLES
SALOON
LODGE
CABINS
MEADOW

ACCESS TO BASEMENT

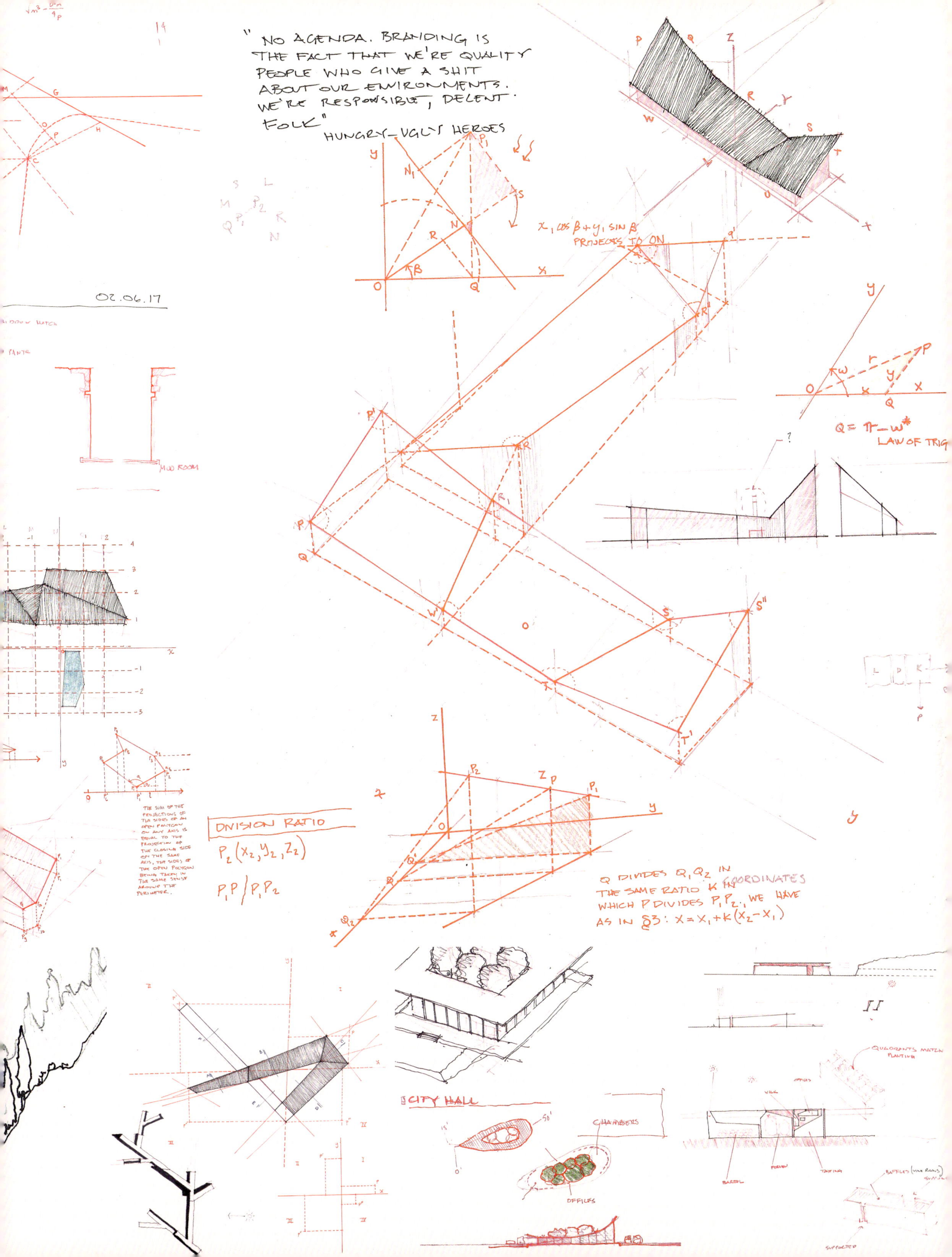
"NO AGENDA. BRANDING IS THE FACT THAT WE'RE QUALITY PEOPLE WHO GIVE A SHIT ABOUT OUR ENVIRONMENTS. WE'RE RESPONSIBLE, DECENT FOLK"
HUNGRY-UGLY HEROES
02.06.17
MUD ROOM
x, cos β + y, sin β PROJECTS TO ON
Q = π − w*
LAW OF TRIG
THE SUM OF THE PROJECTIONS OF THE SIDES OF AN OPEN POLYGON ON ANY AXIS IS EQUAL TO THE PROJECTION OF THE CLOSING SIDE ON THE SAME AXIS, THE SIDES OF THE OPEN POLYGON BEING TAKEN IN THE SAME SENSE AROUND THE PERIMETER.
DIVISION RATIO
P2(x2, y2, z2)
P1P / P1P2
Q DIVIDES Q1Q2 IN THE SAME RATIO K IN COORDINATES WHICH P DIVIDES P1P2. WE HAVE AS IN §3: X = X1 + K(X2 − X1)
CITY HALL
CHAMBERS
OFFICES
QUADRANTS MATCH PLANTING

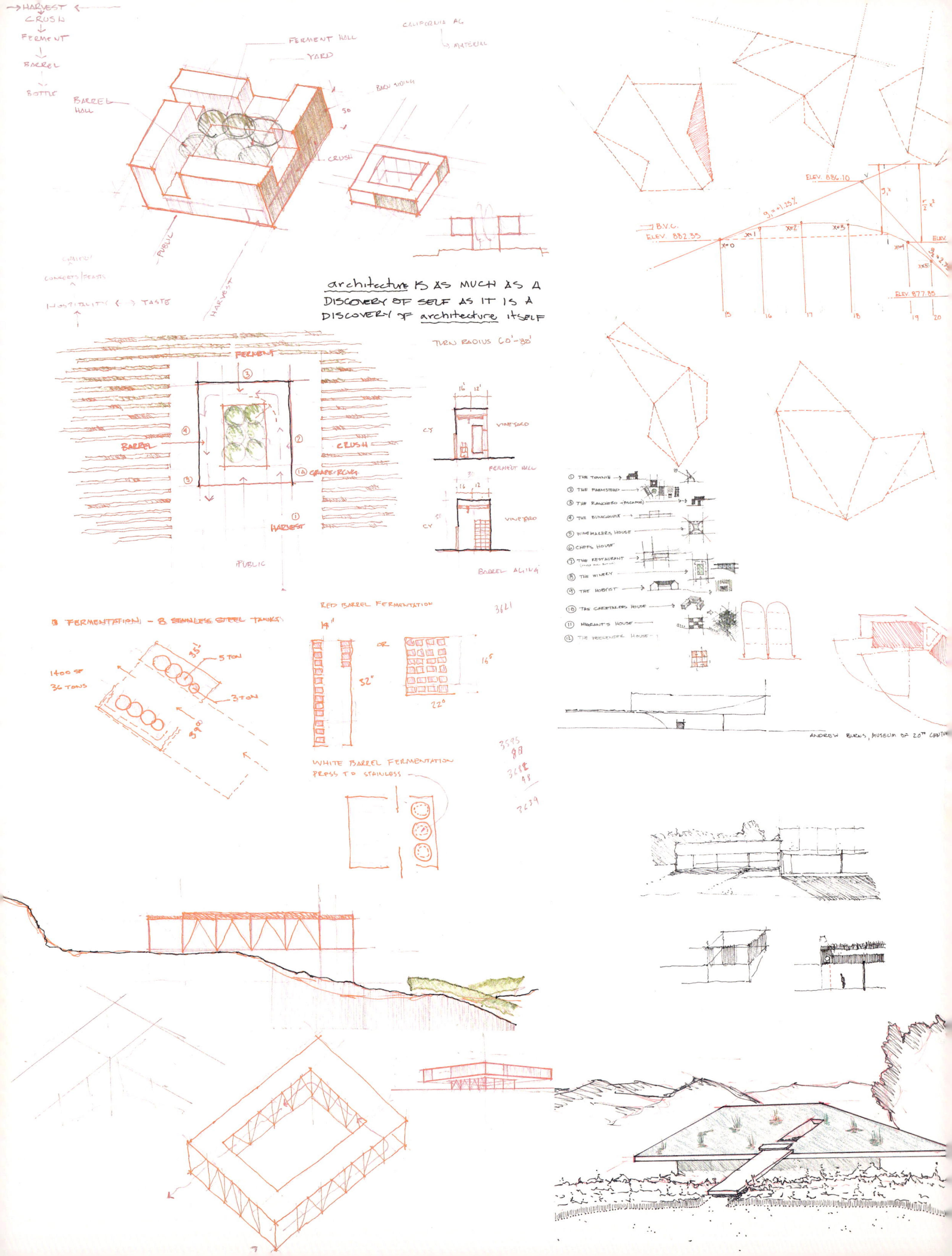
HARVEST
CRUSH
FERMENT
BARREL
BOTTLE
BARREL HALL
FERMENT HALL
YARD
CALIFORNIA AG
MATERIAL
CRUSH
PUBLIC
HARVEST
CONCERTS / FEASTS
HOSPITALITY
TASTE
architecture IS AS MUCH AS A DISCOVERY OF SELF AS IT IS A DISCOVERY OF architecture itself
TURN RADIUS 60'-88'
FERMENT
BARREL
CRUSH
GRAPE RCVG
HARVEST
PUBLIC
VINEYARD
FERMENT HALL
BARREL AGING
B.V.C.
ELEV. 882.35
ELEV. 886.10
ELEV. 877.85
1 THE TOWNIE
2 THE FARMSTEAD
3 THE RANCHERO
4 THE BUNKHOUSE
5 WINEMAKERS HOUSE
6 CHEFS HOUSE
7 THE RESTAURANT
8 THE WINERY
9 THE HOBBYIST
10 THE CARETAKERS HOUSE
11 MIGRANT'S HOUSE
12 THE WEEKENDER HOUSE
FERMENTATION - 8 STAINLESS STEEL TANKS
1400 SF
36 TONS
5 TON
3 TON
RED BARREL FERMENTATION
WHITE BARREL FERMENTATION
PRESS TO STAINLESS
ANDREW BURNS, MUSEUM OF 20TH CENTURY

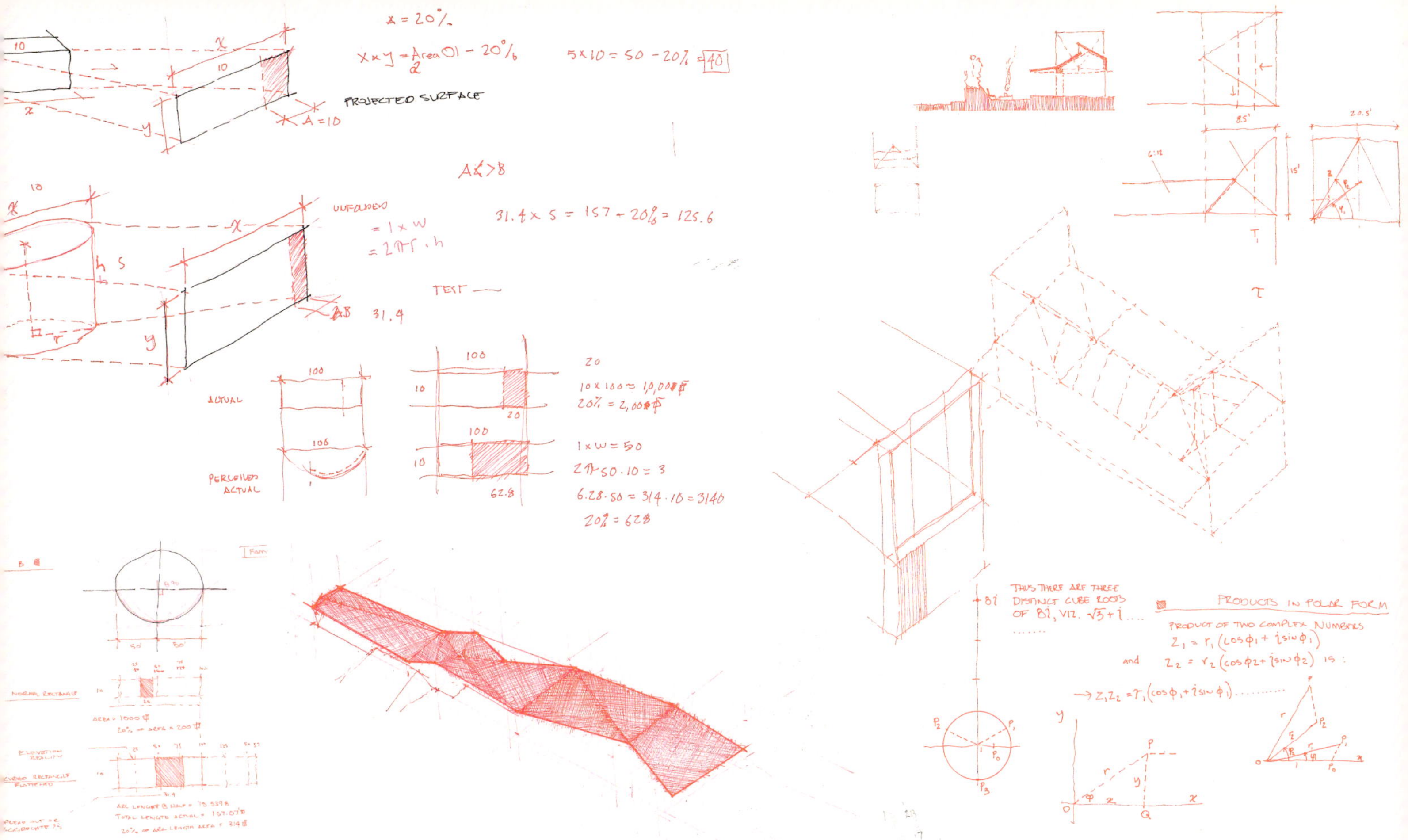

YOU CAN'T SAVE A BAD URBAN PLAN WITH A GOOD BUILDING, WHEREAS A BAD BUILDING CAN EXIST IN A GOOD URBAN PLAN.....

NAPA HAS NO REAL GOOD OR BAD PLAN IT IS REACTING TO BAD DECISION AFTER BAD DECISION, THUS THE CITY HALL CAN BECOME THE GENERATOR OF GOOD DECISIONS TO HAVE A GOOD PLAN WITH GOOD BUILDINGS

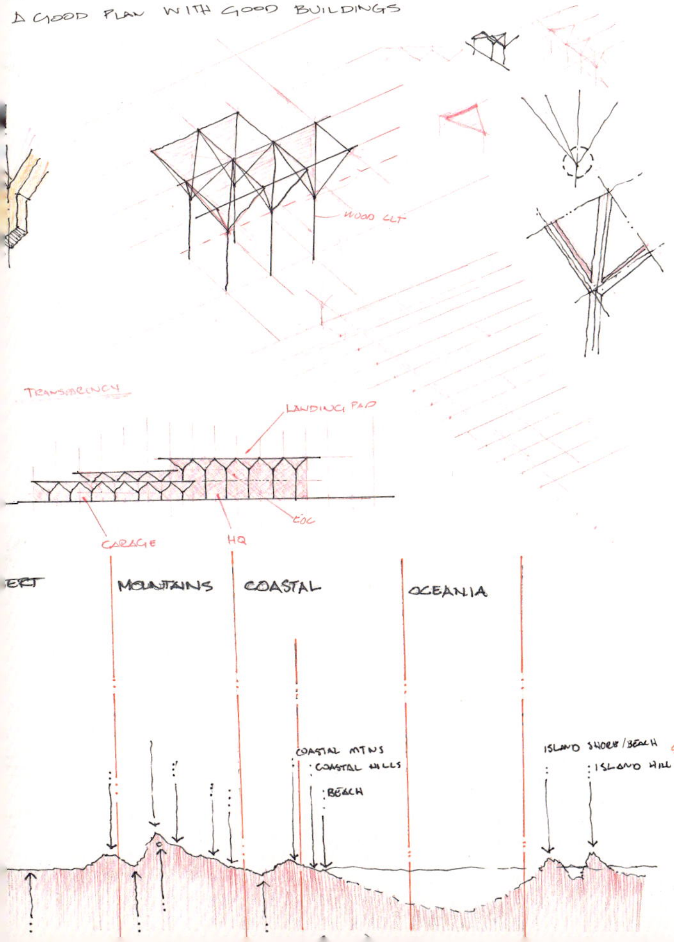

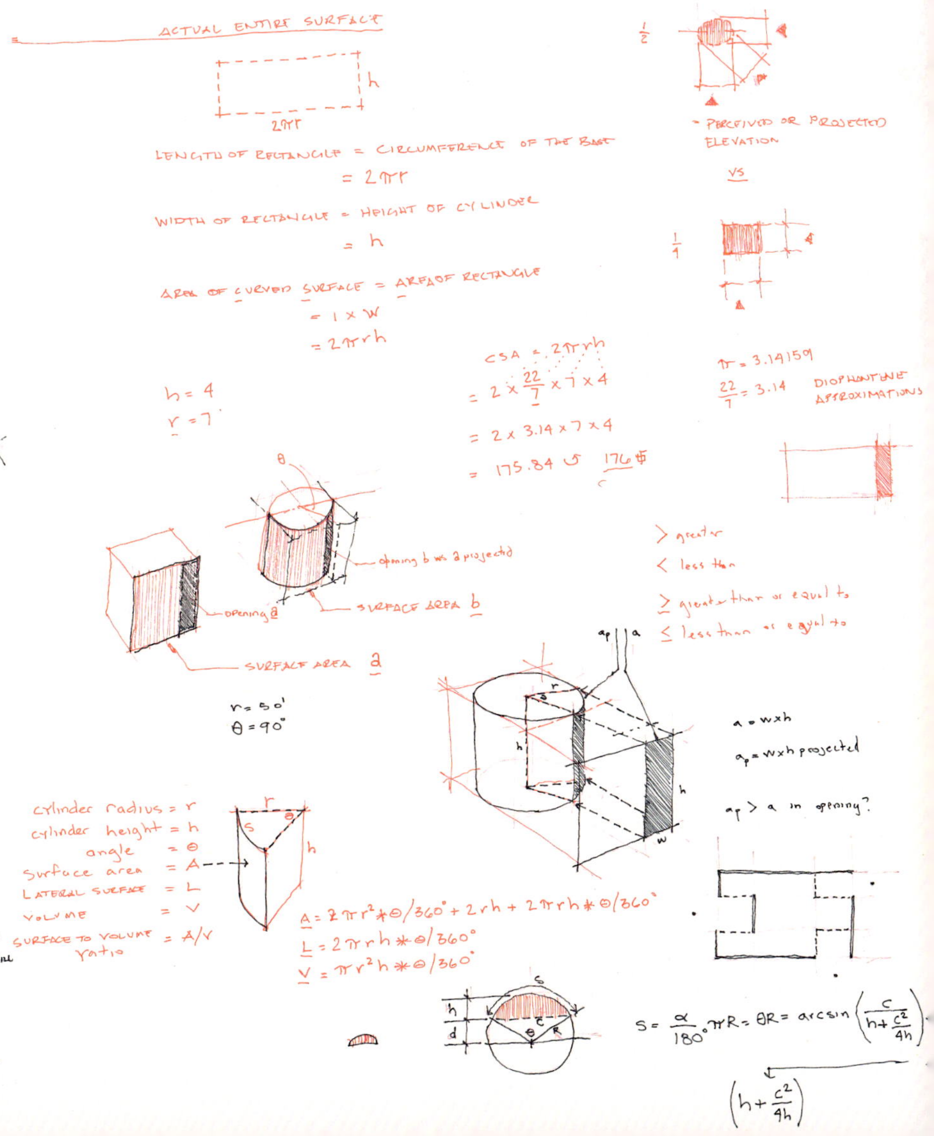

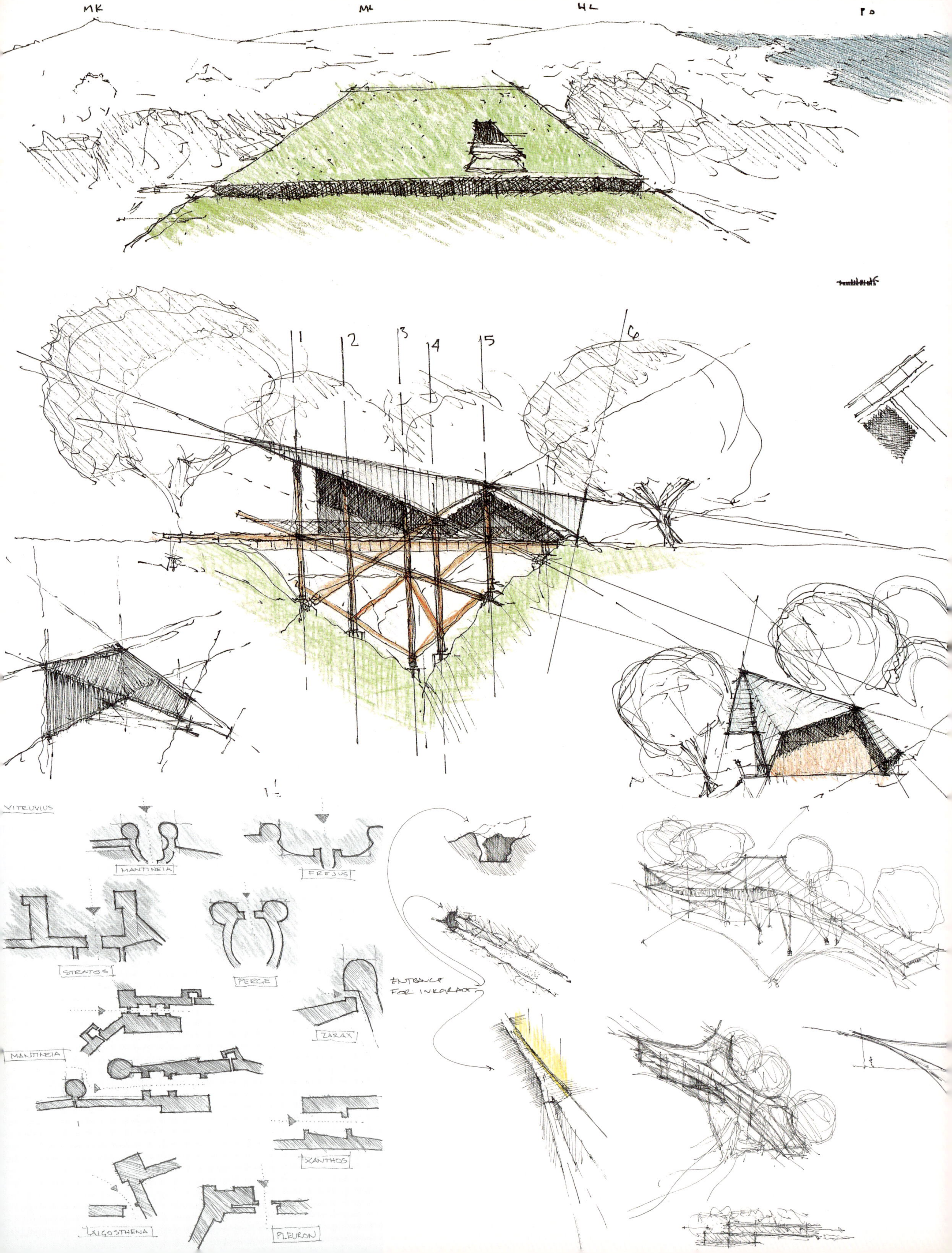
MK
ML
HL
PO
1
2
3
4
5
6
VITRUVIUS
MANTINEIA
FREJUS
STRATOS
PERGE
ZARAX
MANTINEIA
XANTHOS
AIGOSTHENA
PLEURON
ENTRANCE
FOR

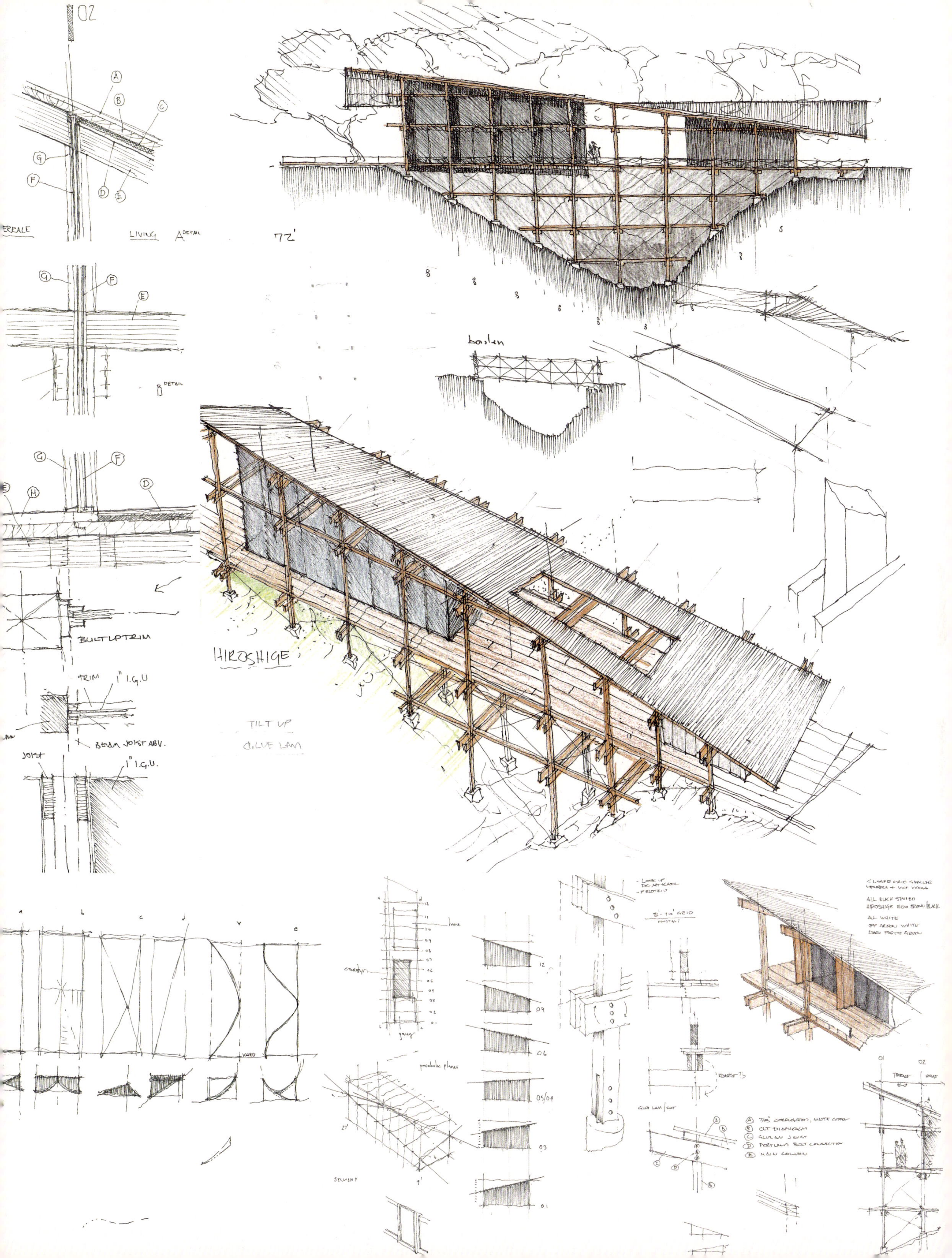
02
LIVING
A DETAIL
B DETAIL
72'
HIROSHIGE
TILT UP
GLUE LAM
TRIM
1" I.G.U
BEAM JOIST ABV.
JOIST
1" I.G.U.
parabolic planes
GLUE LAM / CUT

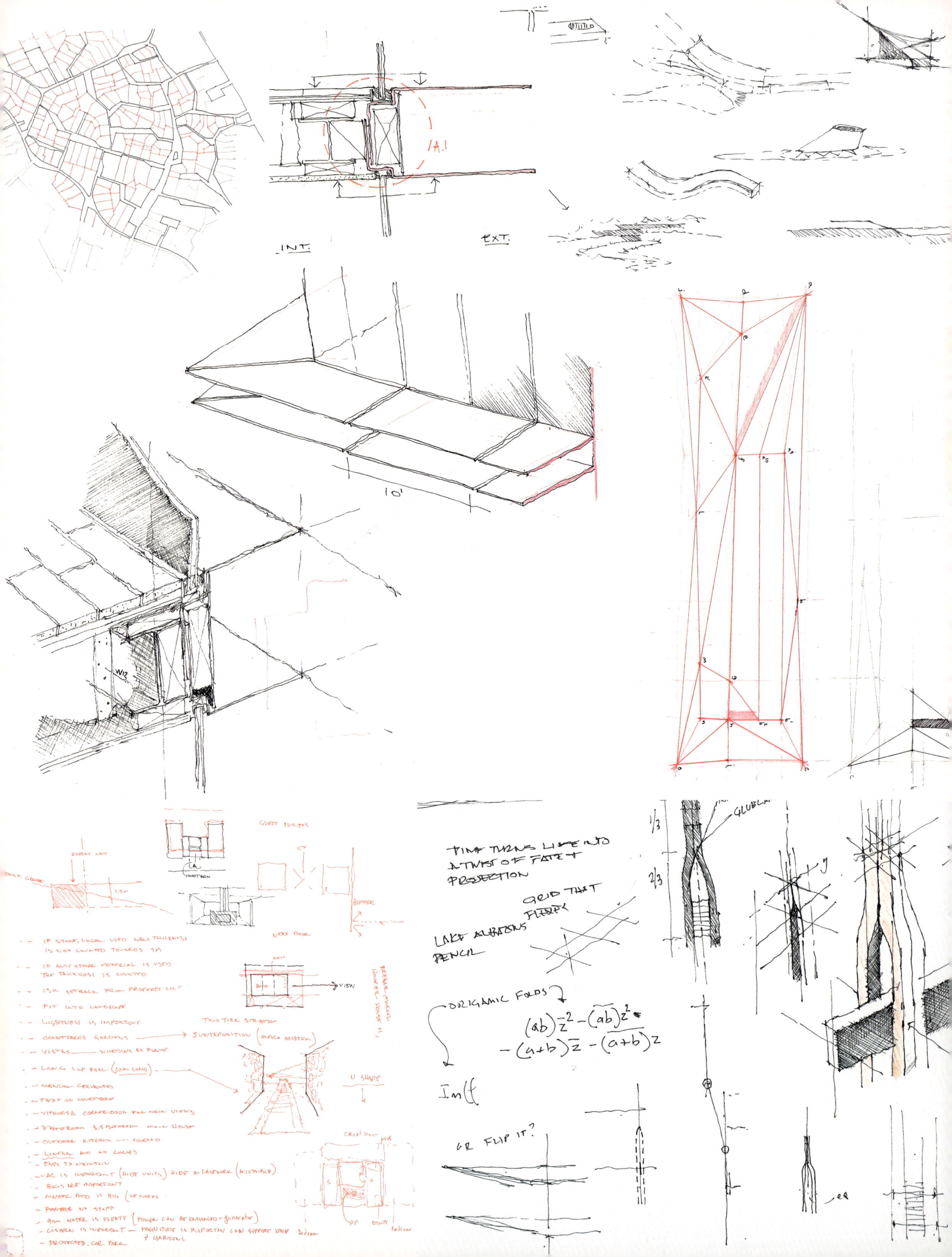

A.1
INT.
EXT.
10'
W12
GUEST BUILDING
COURTYARD
1.5m
BUFFER
NEXT DOOR
IF STONE, LOCAL USED WALL THICKNESS IS NOT COUNTED TOWARDS SM
IF ANY OTHER MATERIAL IS USED THE THICKNESS IS COUNTED
15m SETBACK FROM PROPERTY LINE
FIT INTO LANDSCAPE
LIGHTNESS IS IMPORTANT
COURTYARDS GARDENS
JUXTAPOSITION
VISTAS
LONG LAP POOL (20m LONG)
3 BEDROOM 3.5 BATHROOM MAIN HOUSE
OUTDOOR KITCHEN — COVERED
EASY TO MAINTAIN
AC IS IMPORTANT (HIDE UNITS) HIDE IN CASEWORK (ACCESSIBLE)
BUGS ARE IMPORTANT
MASTER BED IS BIG
POSSIBLE NO STAFF
WATER IS PLENTY (POWER CAN BE ENHANCED - generator)
CISTERN IS IMPORTANT
PROTECTED CAR PARK
TWO TIER SITUATION
VIEW
U SHAPE
FP
UTILITY
TIME TURNS LIFE INTO A TWIST OF FATE + PROJECTION
GRID THAT FLEXES
ORIGAMIC FOLDS
$(ab)\bar{z}^{-2} - (ab)z^{2}$
$-(a+b)\bar{z} - (a+b)z$
OR FLIP IT?
GLUELAM
1/3
2/3

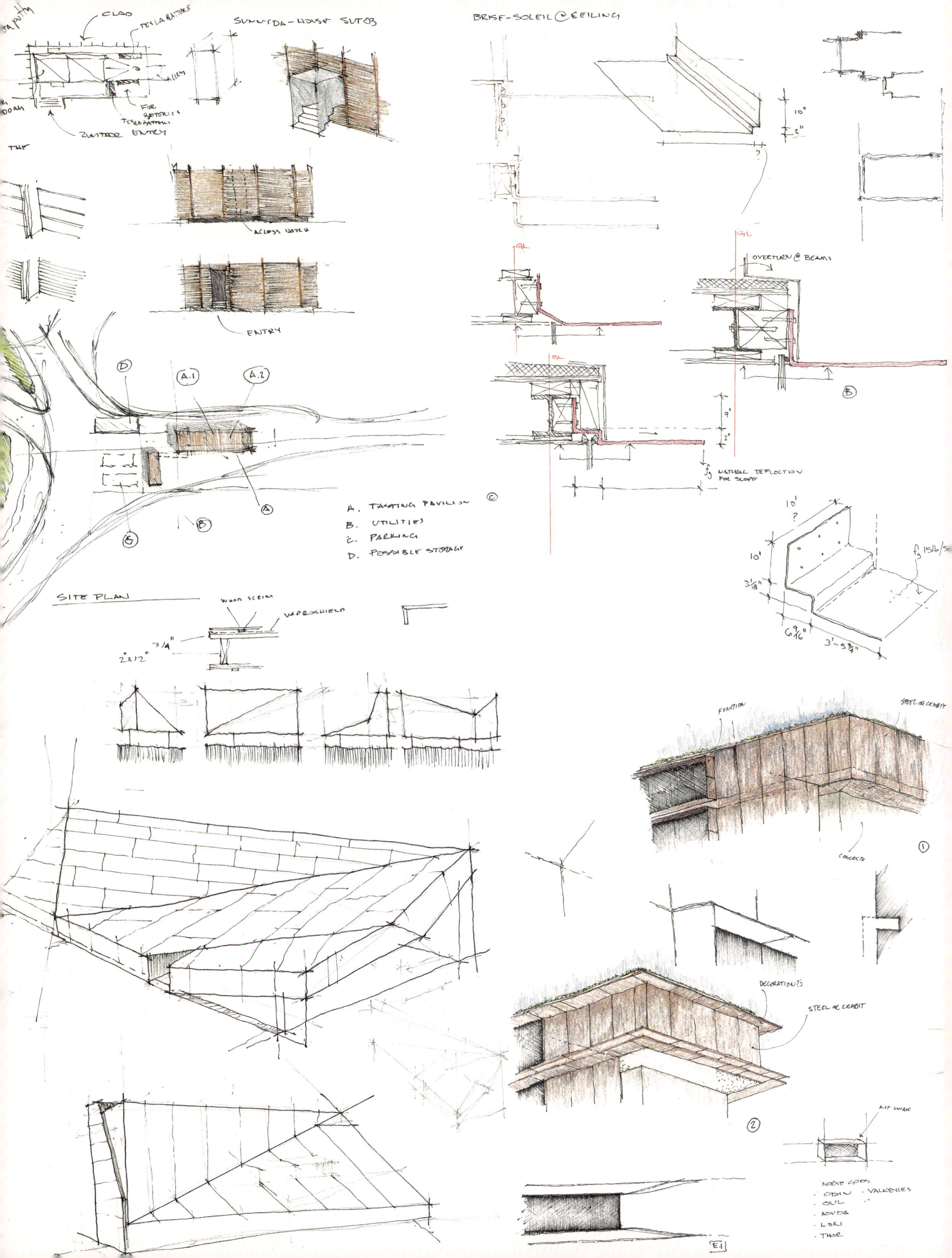

CLAD
BRISE-SOLEIL @ CEILING
ACCESS HATCH
ENTRY
OVERTURN @ BEAMS
NATURAL DEFLECTION FOR SLOPE
A. TASTING PAVILION
B. UTILITIES
C. PARKING
D. POSSIBLE STORAGE
SITE PLAN
WOOD SCRIM
VAPORSHIELD
CONCRETE
NORSE GODS
ODIN
VALKYRIES
LOKI
THOR
E1

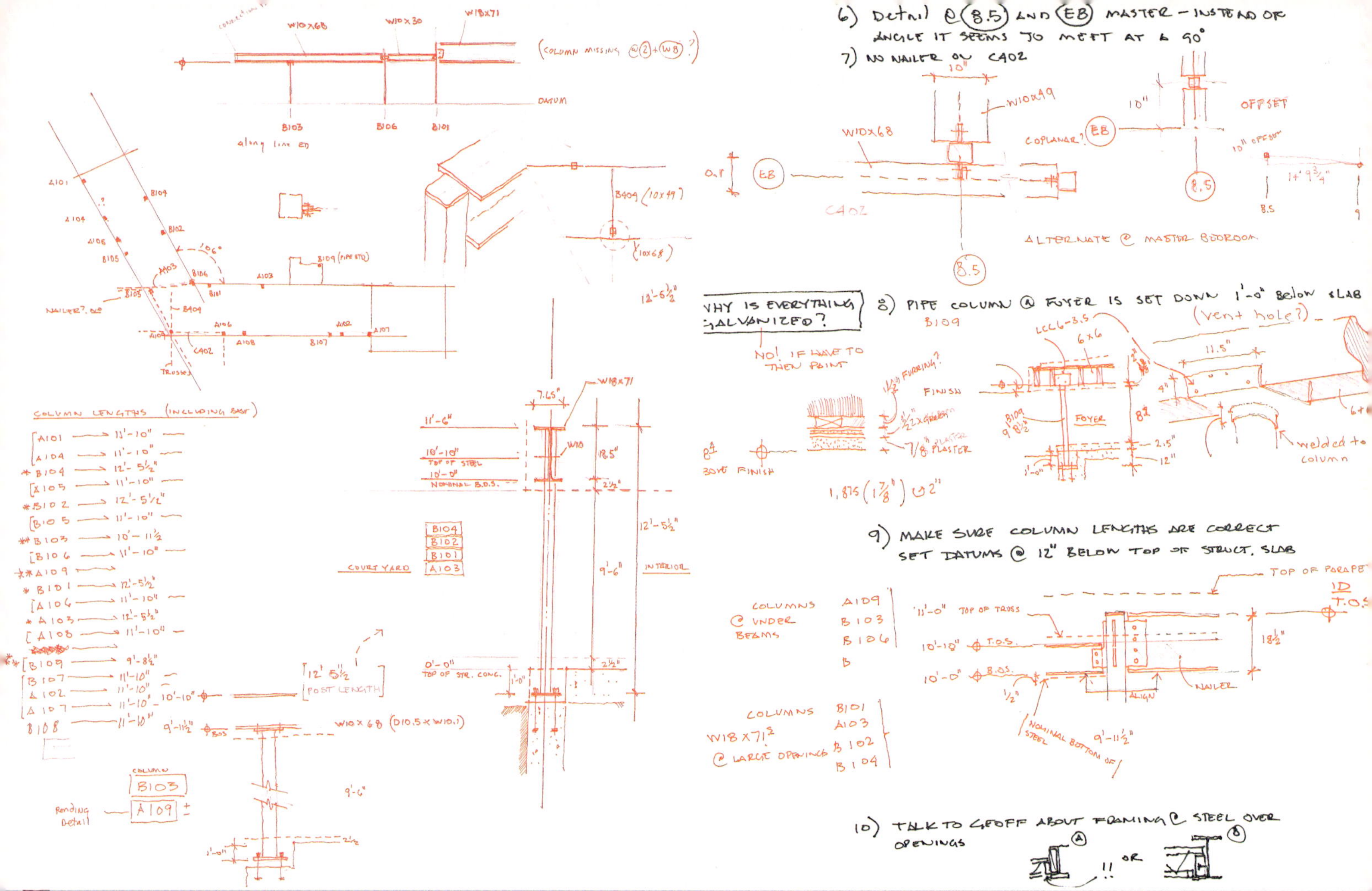
6) Detail @ 8.5 and EB master – instead of angle it seems to meet at a 90°
7) No nailer on C402
ALTERNATE @ MASTER BEDROOM
WHY IS EVERYTHING GALVANIZED?
No! If have to then paint
8) Pipe column @ foyer is set down 1'-0" below slab
(vent hole?)
welded to column
9) Make sure column lengths are correct
Set datums @ 12" below top of struct. slab
COLUMNS @ UNDER BEAMS
COLUMNS W18X71 @ LARGE OPENINGS
10) Talk to Geoff about framing @ steel over openings
COLUMN LENGTHS (INCLUDING BASE)
A101 → 11'-10"
A104 → 11'-10"
B104 → 12'-5½"
X105 → 11'-10"
B102 → 12'-5½"
B105 → 11'-10"
B103 → 10'-11½
B106 → 11'-10"
A109
B101 → 12'-5½"
A106 → 11'-10"
A103 → 12'-5½"
A108 → 11'-10"
B109 → 9'-8½"
B107 → 11'-10"
A102 → 11'-10"
A107 → 11'-10"
B108 → 11'-10"
COURT YARD
INTERIOR
POST LENGTH

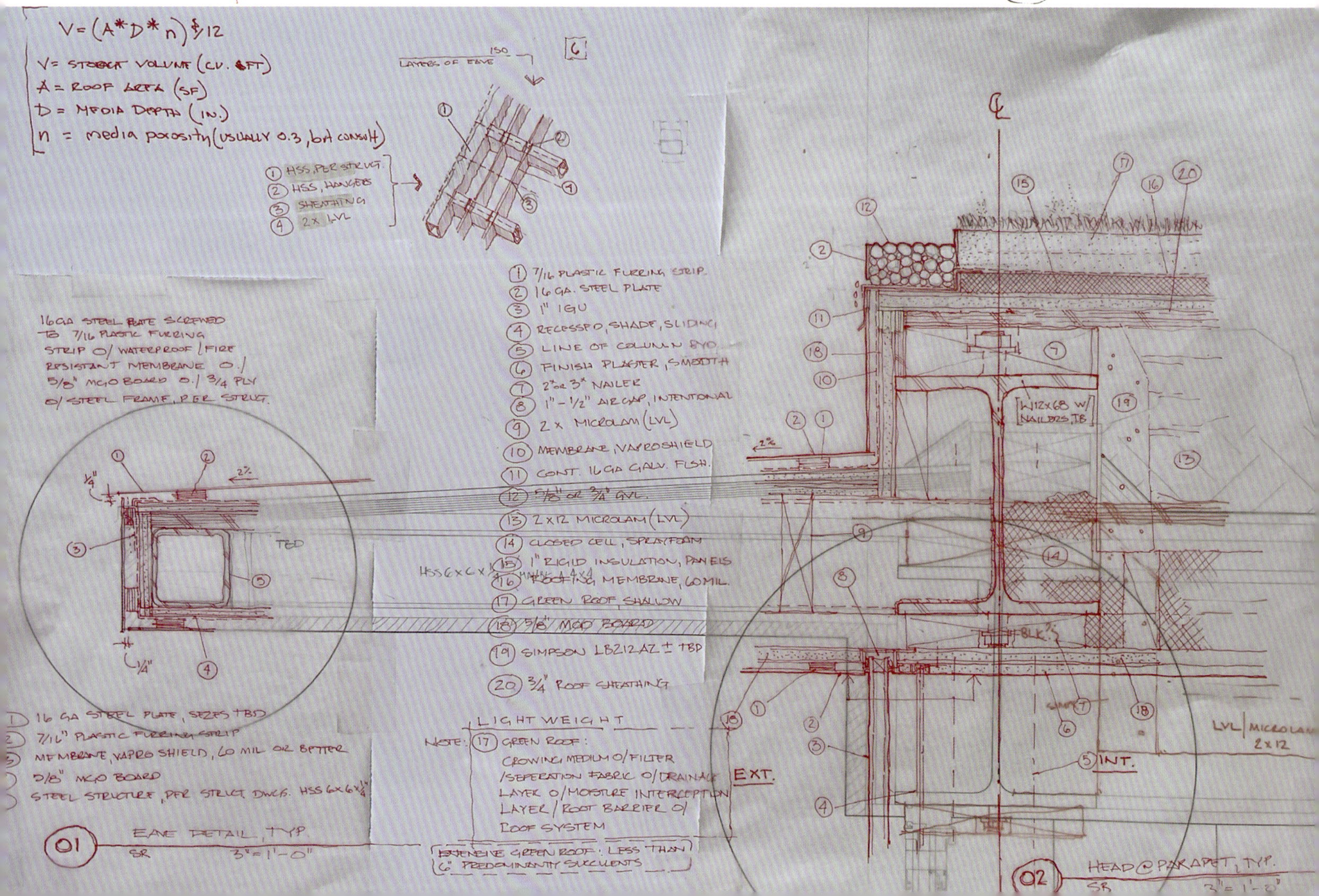
V=(A*D*n)$/12
V= STORAGE VOLUME (CU. FT)
A = ROOF AREA (SF)
D = MEDIA DEPTH (IN.)
n = media porosity (usually 0.3, but consult)
LAYERS OF EAVE
1 HSS, PER STRUCT.
2 HSS, HANGERS
3 SHEATHING
4 2x LVL
16GA STEEL PLATE SCREWED TO 7/16 PLASTIC FURRING STRIP O/ WATERPROOF / FIRE RESISTANT MEMBRANE O/ 5/8" MGO BOARD O/ 3/4 PLY O/ STEEL FRAME, PER STRUCT.
1 7/16 PLASTIC FURRING STRIP
2 16 GA. STEEL PLATE
3 1" IGU
4 RECESSED, SHADE, SLIDING
5 LINE OF COLUMN BYD.
6 FINISH PLASTER, SMOOTH
7 2"x3" NAILER
8 1"-1/2" AIR GAP, INTENTIONAL
9 2x MICROLAM (LVL)
10 MEMBRANE, VAPROSHIELD
11 CONT. 16GA GALV. FLSH.
12 5/8" OR 3/4" GVL.
13 2x12 MICROLAM (LVL)
14 CLOSED CELL, SPRAYFOAM
15 1" RIGID INSULATION, PANELS
16 ROOFING MEMBRANE, 60MIL.
17 GREEN ROOF, SHALLOW
18 5/8" MGO BOARD
19 SIMPSON LBZ12AZ ± TBD
20 3/4 ROOF SHEATHING
W12x68 W/ NAILERS, TBD
1 16 GA STEEL PLATE, SIZES TBD
2 7/16" PLASTIC FURRING STRIP
3 MEMBRANE, VAPRO SHIELD, 60 MIL OR BETTER
4 5/8" MGO BOARD
5 STEEL STRUCTURE, PER STRUCT DWGS. HSS 6x6x¼
LIGHT WEIGHT
NOTE: 17 GREEN ROOF: GROWING MEDIUM O/ FILTER / SEPERATION FABRIC O/ DRAINAGE LAYER O/ MOISTURE INTERCEPTION LAYER / ROOT BARRIER O/ ROOF SYSTEM
EXTENSIVE GREEN ROOF: LESS THAN 6" PREDOMINANTLY SUCCULENTS
EXT.
INT.
01 EAVE DETAIL, TYP. SR 3"=1'-0"
02 HEAD @ PARAPET, TYP. SR

04.01.21

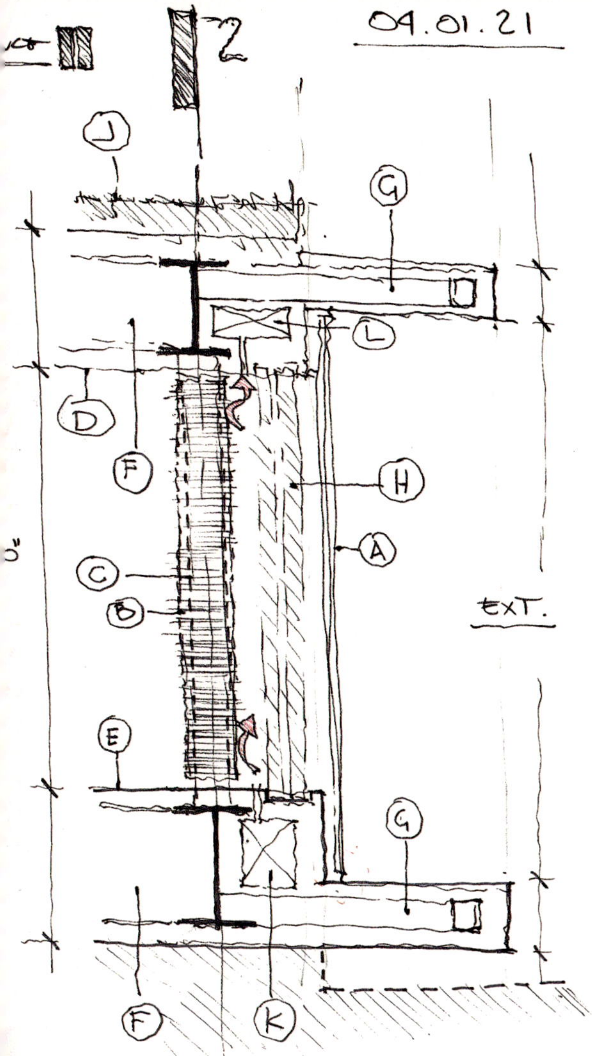

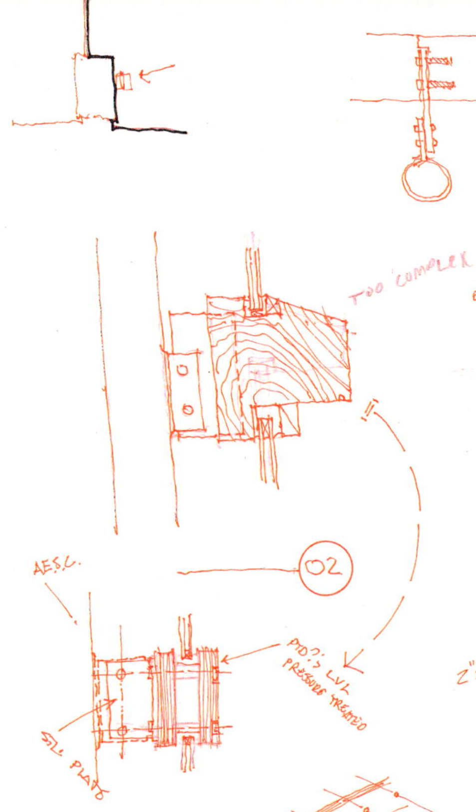

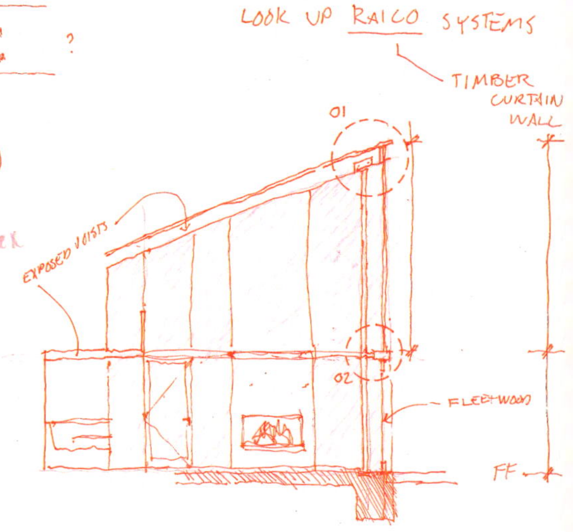

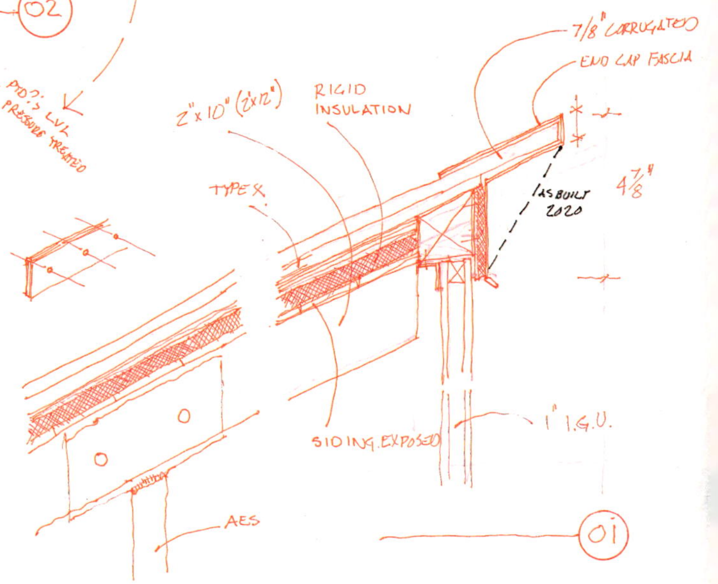

'IDEOLOGICAL ACOLYTES'
+ IDENTITY POLITICS

HEIARCHY OF COMPETENCE

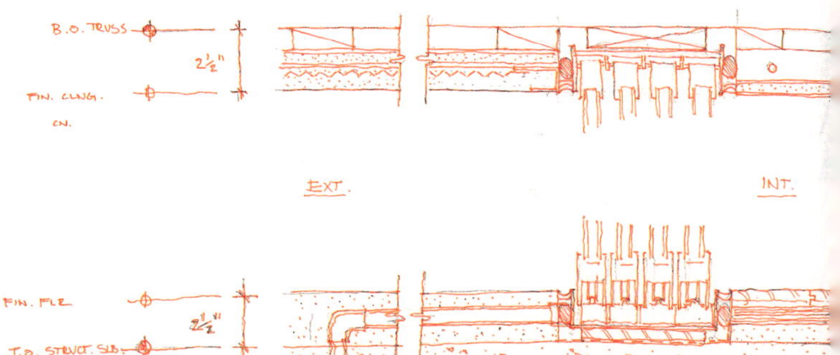

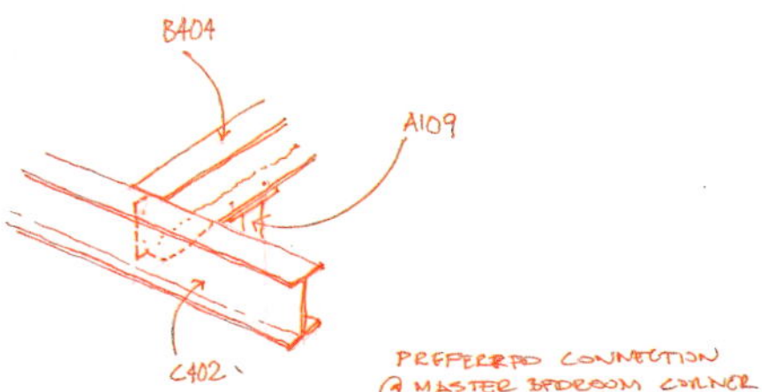

PREFERRED CONNECTION @ MASTER BEDROOM CORNER

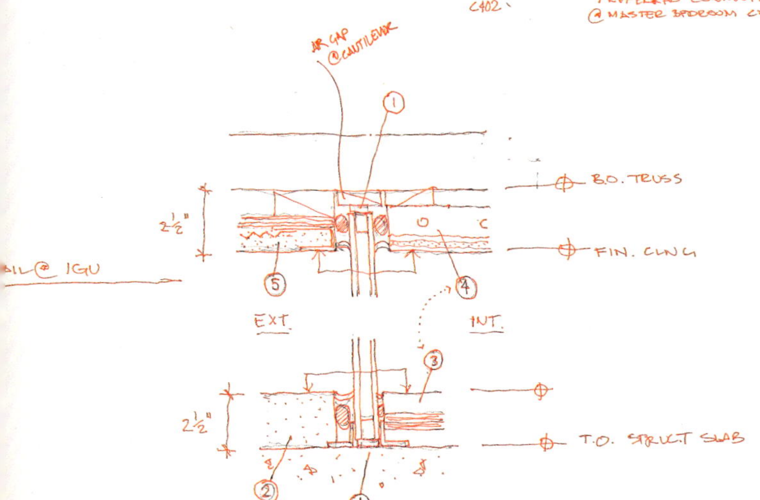

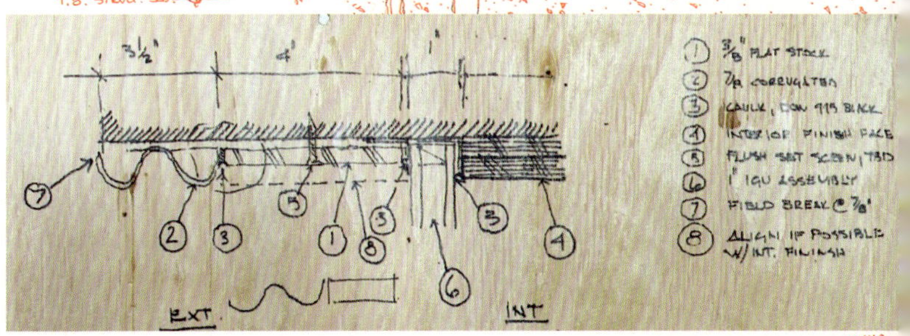

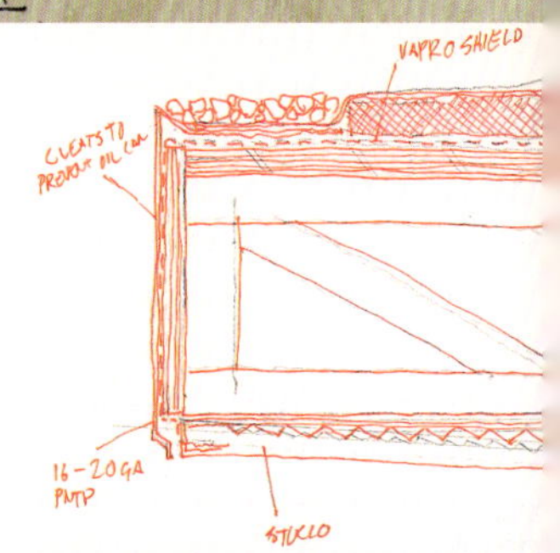

FIRST INSTALLED: 1" GLAZING (IGU)
2 1/2" TOPPING SLAB
THIRD INSTALLED: WOOD FLOORING OVER PLY OVER 1" OVERLAY (SELF LEVELING)
FOURTH INSTALLED: MESSANA PANEL OVER NAILERS/FURRING ATTACHED TO B.O. TRUSS
FIFTH INSTALLED: SMOOTH COAT INTEGRAL COLOR STUCCO O/ MGO O/ FURRING

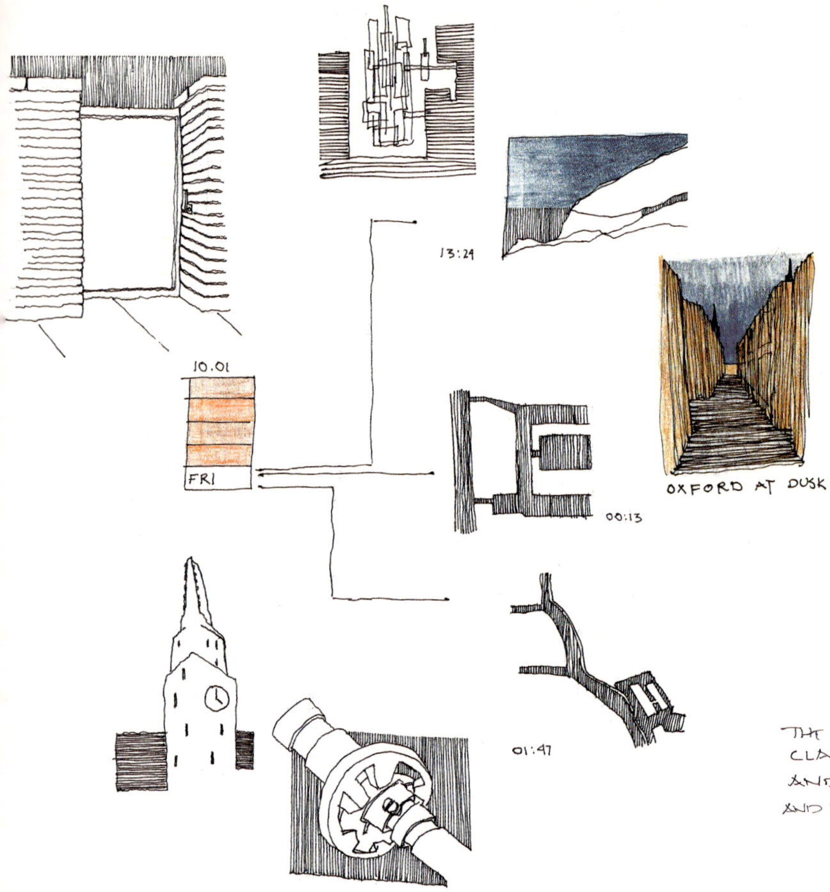

NOTES:

ALHAMBRA IS A PLACE, THAT, AT FIRST GLANCE OR EXPERIENCED WITH REGARDS TO THE LIGHT, THE MATERIALS, OR THE PROPORTIONS SEEMS TO BE PERFECT.

I BELIEVE THAT IS THE SECRET OF THIS PLACE. ONCE YOU SIT AND REALLY LOOK, YOU CAN SEE ITS IMPERFECTION... THE SLIGHT ANGLE OF THE COURT YARDS, WHICH ARE SUPPOSED BE ABSOLUTE, ARE NOT PERFECT.

THE IMPERFECTION IS NOT WABI-SABI YET THE IMPERFECTION IS CALCULATED. (B) I BELIEVE ALL OF THEM SAW THIS (A) AND I BELIEVE IT IS THE ESSENCE OF WHAT MAKES THEIR WORK PERFECTLY IMPERFECT AND BEAUTIFUL.'

EVERY PERSON THAT HAS WALKED HERE THINKS THAT THIS PLACE IS BEAUTIFUL. THE REASON WHY IS SET AND ANCHORED IN THE SOMBER ACCIDENTAL 'MISTAKES' IN THE GEOMETRY.

THE MATERIAL OF RAMMED EARTH, ROMAN BRICK, CLAY TILES, WOOD TIMBER (CYPRESS IT SEEMS), IRON AND PLANTS (ALL HAVE PURPOSE) MARBLE, PLASTER, AND PIGMENT.

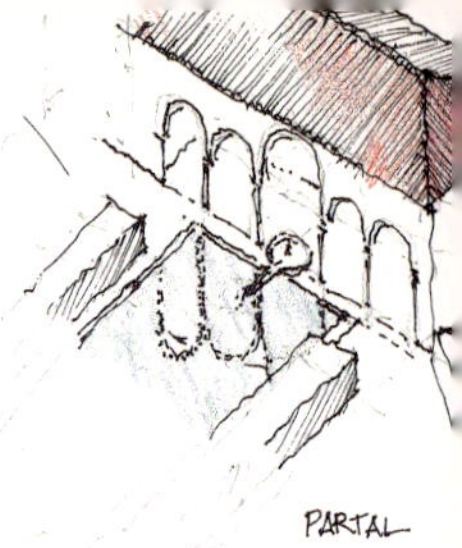

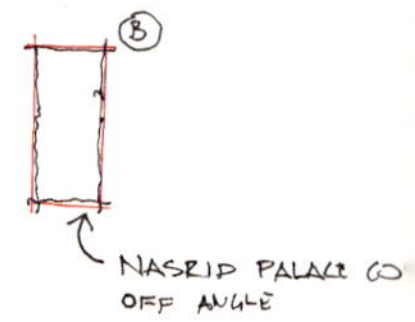

(A) LOOS
CORBU
WRIGHT
MIES
HERZOG + DEMEURON
RCR
BARRAGAN

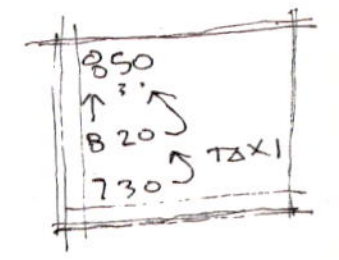

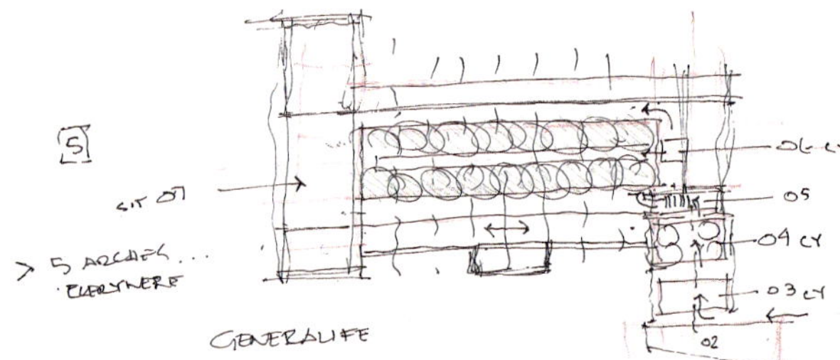

01

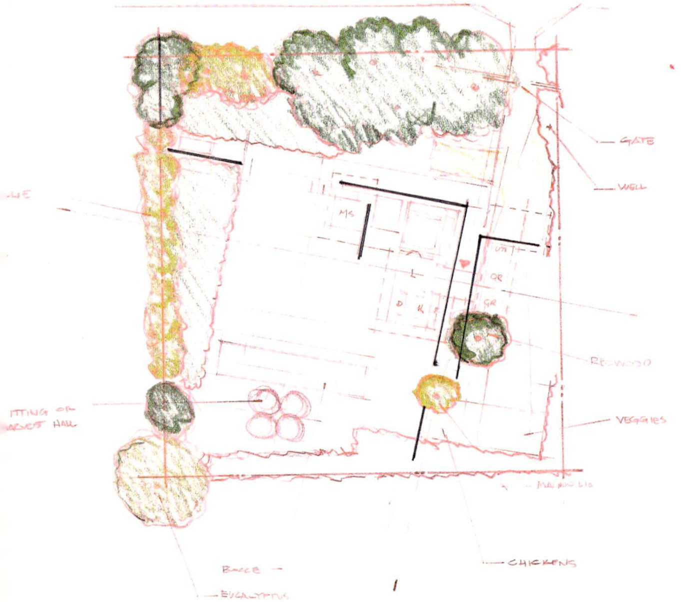

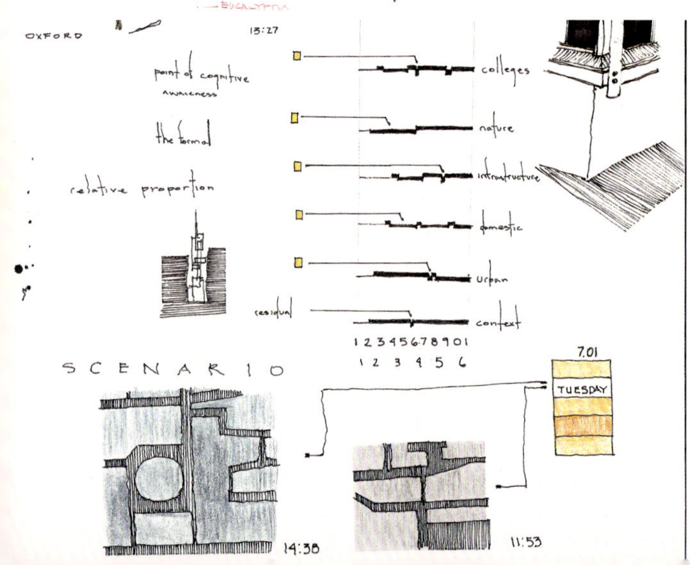

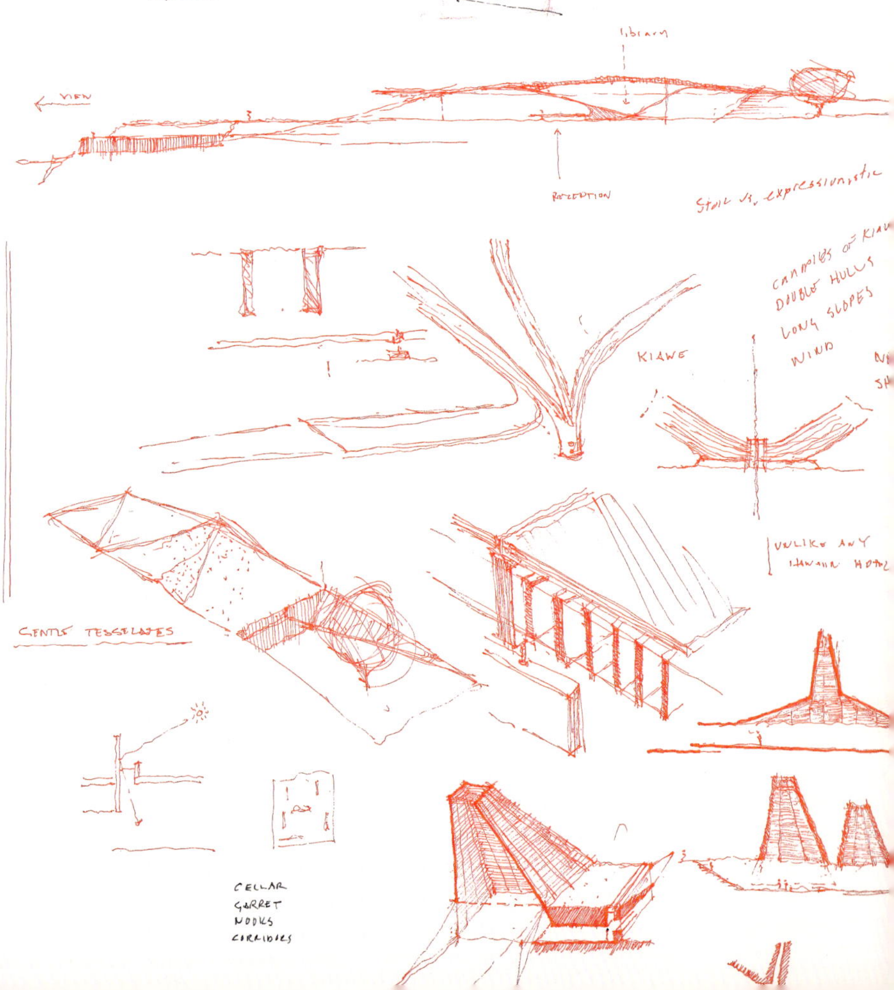

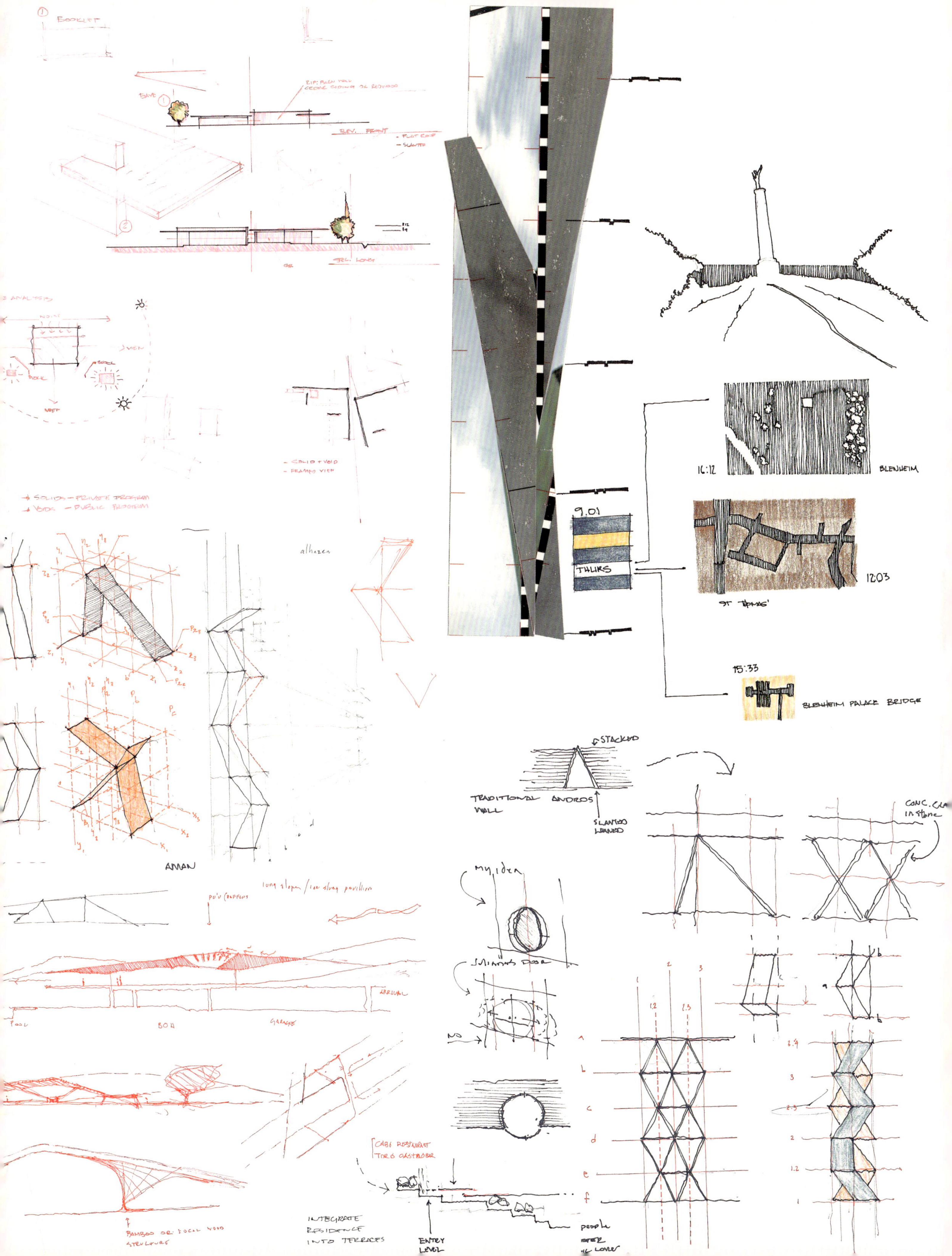
BOOKLET
ELEV. FRONT
ELEV. LONG
SOLID + VOID
FRAMED VIEW
SOLIDS - PRIVATE PROGRAM
VOIDS - PUBLIC PROGRAM
alhazen
AMAN
ARRIVAL
POOL
BOH
GARAGE
BAMBOO OR LOCAL WOOD STRUCTURE
INTEGRATE RESIDENCE INTO TERRACES
ENTRY LEVEL
9.01
THURS
16:12
BLENHEIM
12:03
ST THOMAS'
15:33
BLENHEIM PALACE BRIDGE
STACKED
TRADITIONAL WALL
ANDROS
SLANTED LEANED
my idea
in stone

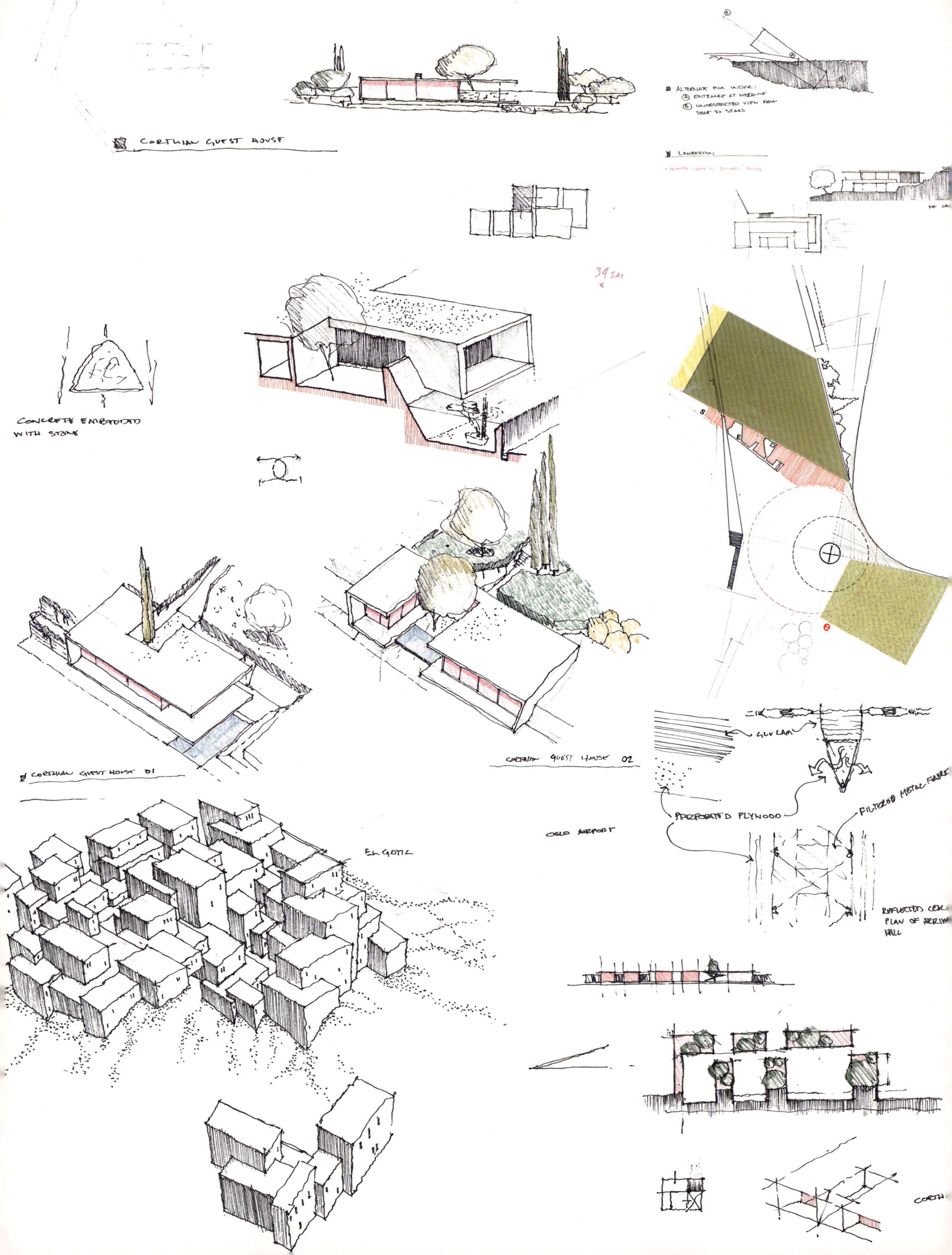
CORTHIAN GUEST HOUSE
LAMBERTON
34 sm
CONCRETE EMBEDDED WITH STONE
CORTHIAN GUEST HOUSE 01
CORTHIAN GUEST HOUSE 02
GLULAM
PERFORATED PLYWOOD
OSLO AIRPORT
EL GOTIC

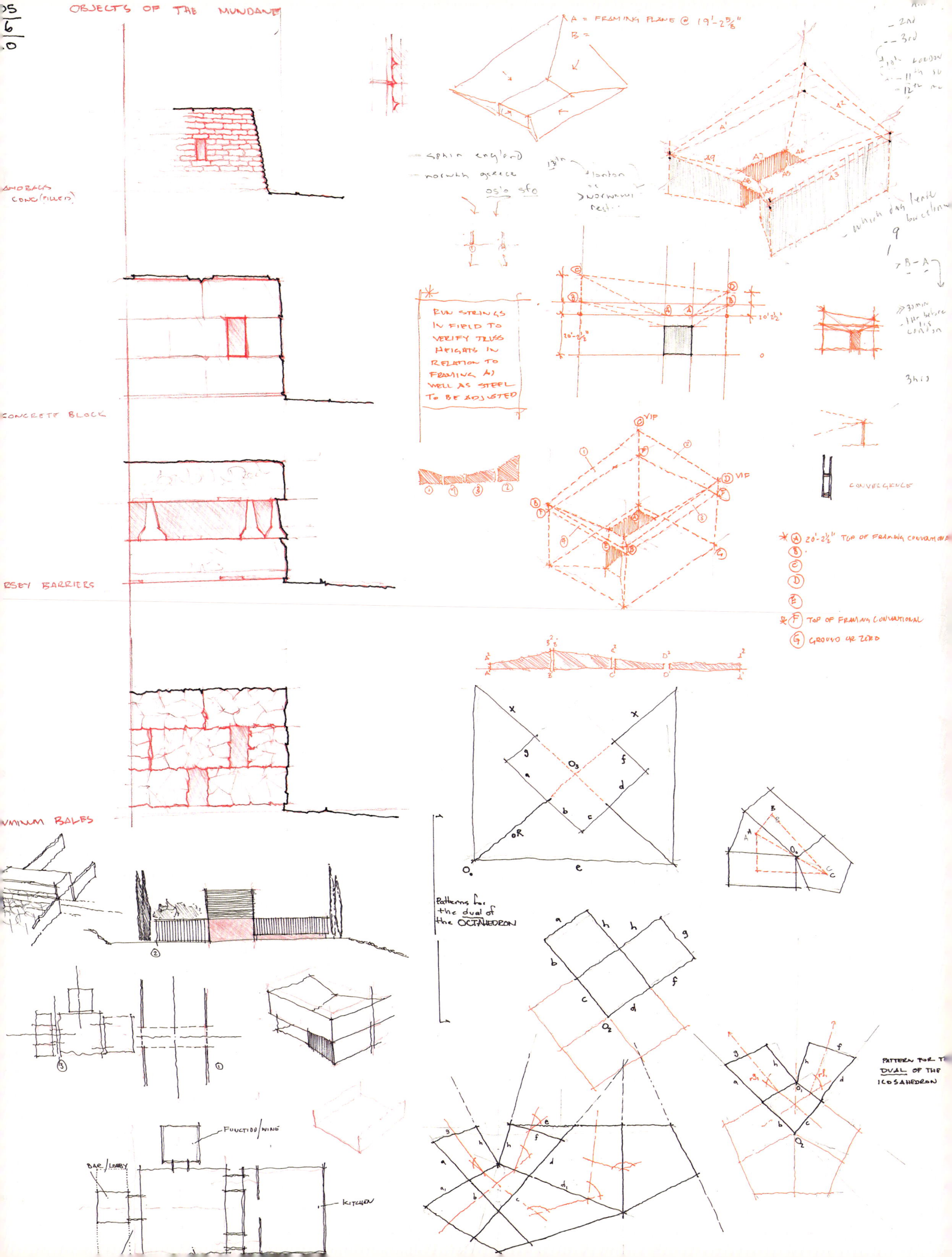
OBJECTS OF THE MUNDANE
A = FRAMING PLANE @ 19'-2 5/8"
B =
spain england
norway greece
os'lo sfo
london
CONCRETE BLOCK
RSEY BARRIERS
RUN STRINGS IN FIELD TO VERIFY TRUSS HEIGHTS IN RELATION TO FRAMING AS WELL AS STEEL TO BE ADJUSTED
20'-2 1/2"
VIP
CONVERGENCE
which day leave barcelona
A 20'-2 1/2" TOP OF FRAMING CONVENTIONAL
F TOP OF FRAMING CONVENTIONAL
G GROUND OR ZERO
Patterns for the dual of the OCTAHEDRON
PATTERN FOR THE DUAL OF THE ICOSAHEDRON
FUNCTION/WINE
BAR/LOBBY
KITCHEN

RUTHERFORD

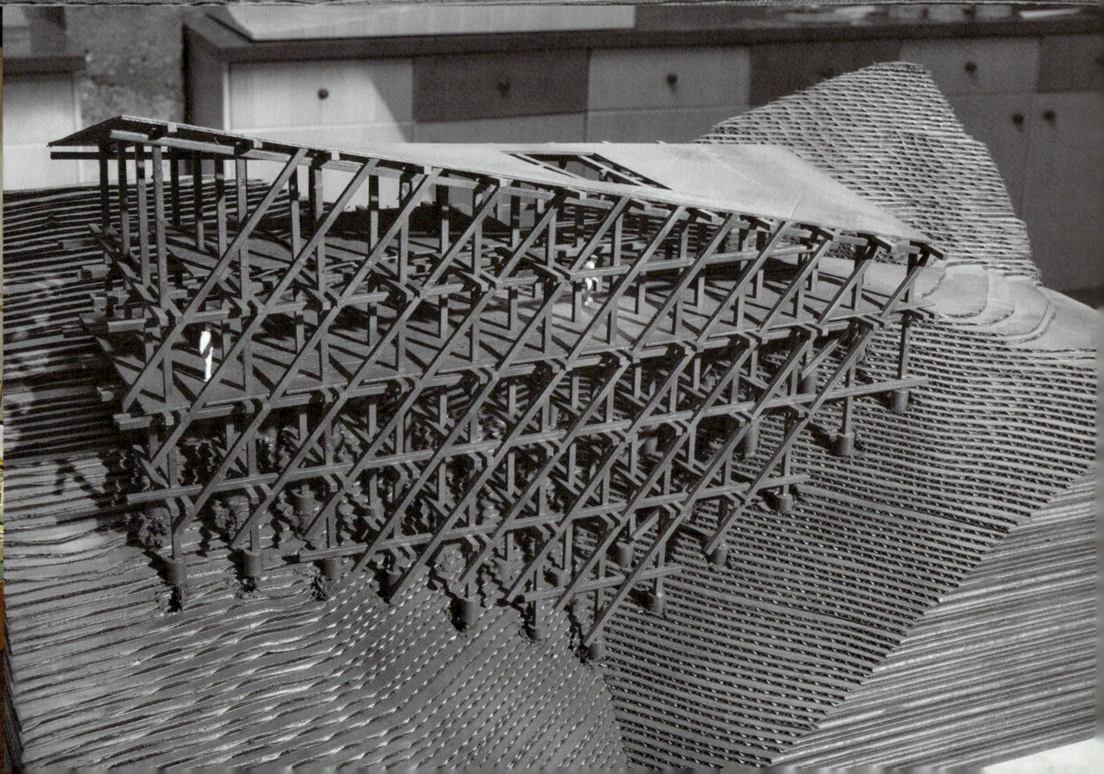

BARTON RESIDENCE

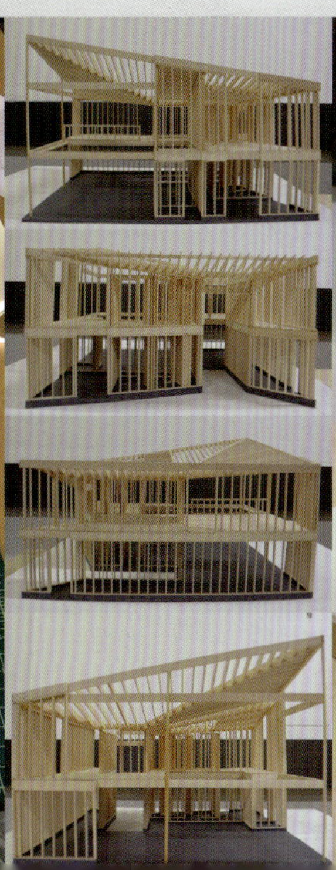

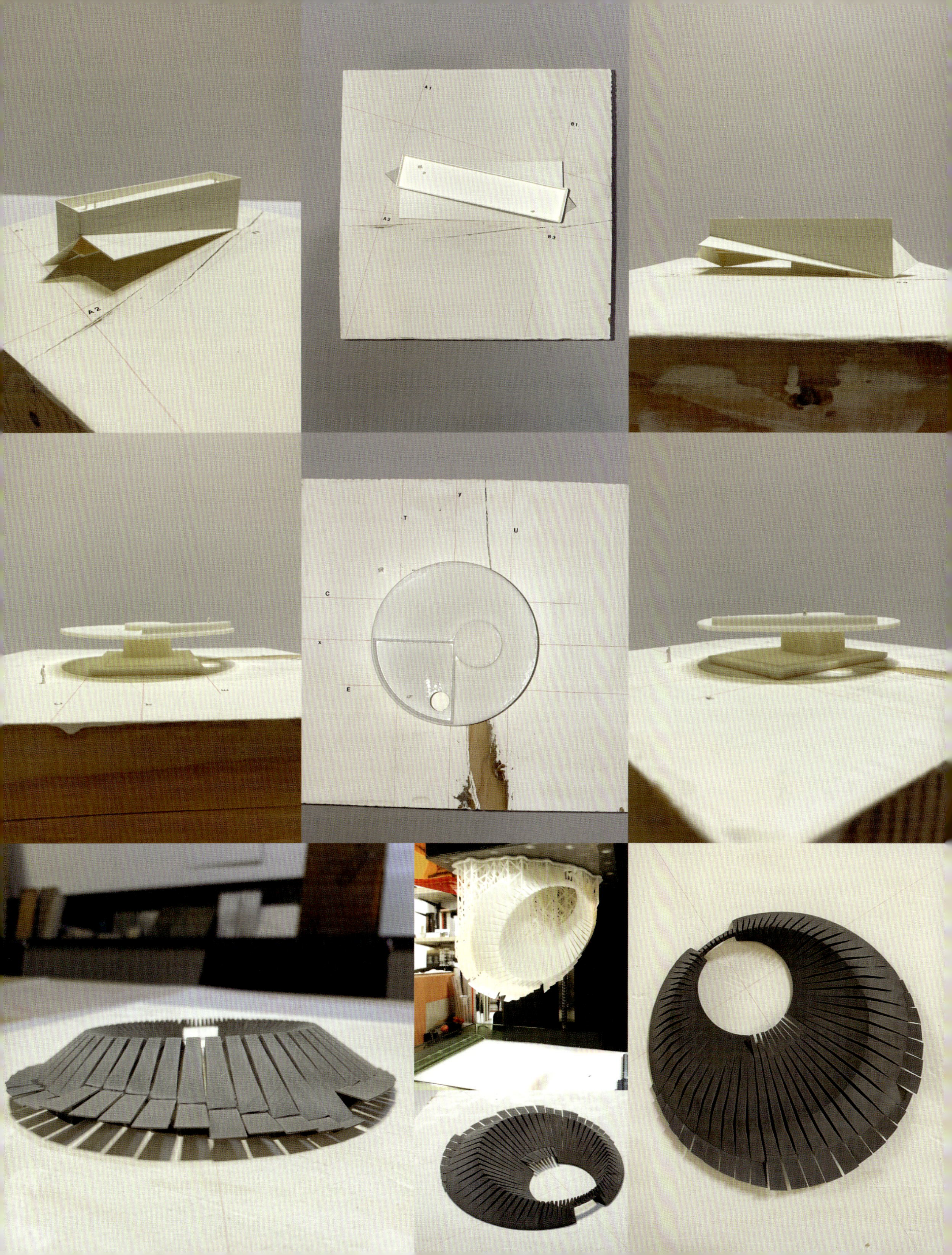
A2
A1
B1
A2
B3
T
y
U
C
x
E

Pacific
Wood
Laminates

PRECISION
800-922-3302

Selected Works

swift ranch

Knights Valley, California 2011
completed, 2019
featured,
> january 2022 arch. digest

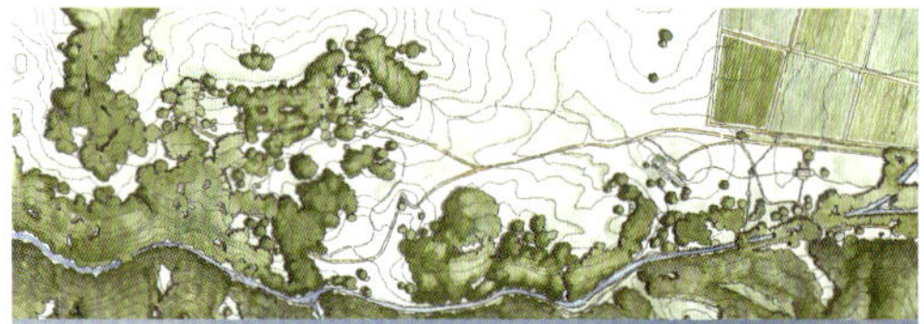

A legacy self sustaining ranch design & master plan for a family from Manhatten New York.

project team:	Brandon Jørgensen
water color:	Atelier Jørgensen
photos:	Laura Resen

oak knoll residence

Napa Valley, California 2013
completed, 2014
featured,

> june 2015 cottages & garden
> june 2015 arch daily
> june 2015 hypebeast
> july 2015 dezeen

A 5,500sf residence for a retired couple from Texas. The house shelters itself from the busy country road while framing the views of the hills beyond.

project team:	Brandon Jørgensen
photos:	Joe Fletcher

coastal retreat

Trinidad, California 2012 - 2013

A getaway from the fast life of New York for a lovely couple who fell in love with the north coast of California.

project team:	Brandon Jørgensen
rendering:	Atelier Jørgensen & Claudio Campra

pumphouse studio

Berkeley, California 2000
completed, 2001

A small studio/residence reclaimed from an old water storage tank and pump room from the original farm on the property built in 1898.

project team: Brandon Jørgensen, Jake LaChapelle, & William W Jørgensen
photos: Brandon Jørgensen

jørgensen residence

Napa, California 2014
completed, 2016
featured,

> march 2016 wall street journal
> march 2016 new york times
> march 2016 hypebeast

A mid century rebuild & refurbishment of the Barr Residence, designed by Walter Thomas Brooks originally. Interior and Landscape Design with structural upgrades to match original rehab and landscape design, by Jørgensen

project team: Brandon Jørgensen & Kathryn K. Jørgensen
photos: Joe Fletcher

dry creek estate

Napa, California 2016

A 7,000 square foot retreat for a family from Los Angeles, designed as a respite from the frenetic pace of hollywood.

project team: Brandon Jørgensen, Brett Collins
rendering: Claudio Campre

california farnsworth

Napa, California 2015

A 600 square foot guest house design using custom redwood CLT for the structure as an homage to Mies Van Der Rohes steel structure at the Farnsworth house.

project team: Brandon Jørgensen
renderings: Claudio Campre

jones redux

Sunol, California 2016

A 1,500 square foot residential design for a young family designed to be built using "off the shelf" materials with close zero waste for very modest budget.

project team: Brandon Jørgensen
model photo: Joe Fletcher
renderings: Claudio Campre

montecito forest residence

Napa Valley, California 2016

completed, 2021

A 3,600sf residence for a retired couple from Rhode Island. The house shelters itself from the street being situated on the middle of the hillside while framing the views of the vineyards beyond.

project team: Brandon Jørgensen, Jonathan Solis
renderings: Claudio Campra & Atelier Jørgensen

von bates residence

Napa, California 2017

A 1,600sf residence addition for a couple in Napa, one a maker and the other a landscape designer. The addition uses their love of the natural light as the driver for the new space to enjoy with their two children.

project team: Brandon Jørgensen
renderings: Claudio Campra

trinity overlook (resilient 001)

Sonoma, California 2017

This 2,780sf residence design was one of several resulting from the 2017 fires in Napa and Sonoma County - families who lost everything in these fires colloborated with our practice to re-build a hardened and resilient new residence.

project team: Brandon Jørgensen
renderings: Claudio Campra

glen ellen retreat (resilient 002)

Glen Ellen, California 2017

This 4,450sf residence design was the second of several resulting from the 2017 fires in Napa and Sonoma County the design of this rebuild aims towards a hardened and resilient new residence.

project team: Brandon Jørgensen
renderings: Claudio Campra

bayview farm
Korthiou, Andros, Greece 2018 –

A 4,500sf residence for a family who reside in London and eventually will shift their life to the island of Andros, Greece. The farm is to be self sustaining and protected from the environment of cold strong winds in the winter and the hot mediteranean sun in the summer.

project team: Brandon Jørgensen, Jonathan Solis
renderings: Claudio Campra

stokes canyon residence
Calabasas, California 2018 – 2019

A 48,500sf residence for a couple and their family from Calbasas, California. The house takes the position that bridges itself across its site versus being placed on a typical tract house scraped flat lot, lightly touching the ground.

project team: Brandon Jørgensen, Lisha Zhang, Dora Tam, Jonathan Solis, Petra Kustrin, & Jalil Peraza
renderings: Claudio Campra & Atelier Jørgensen

mount veeder outpost (resilient 003)
Napa, California 2018
completed, 2020
featured,

> nov / dec 2021 dwell mag
> dec 2021 arch digest
> feb 2022 hypebeast
> mar 2022 designboom
> mar 2022 archdaily
> mar 2022 hypebeast

A 2,316sf residence for a retired couple from Rhode Island. The house shelters itself from the street being situated on the middle of the hillside while framing the views of the vineyards beyond.

project team: Brandon Jørgensen, Lisha Zhang, Dora Tam, Jonathan Solis
photos: Joe Fletcher, Douglas Friedman

casa B
Los Angeles, California 2018

A 2,500sf residence for a young family who relocated from europe to be closer to family and friends. This house is set on the hills above downtown Los Angeles with views extending to the Pacific Ocean. Casa B is designed to be a humble extension of their life.

project team: Brandon Jørgensen, Farzad Morè with Michael Brown
renderings: Claudio Campra

sky hut (resilient 004)

Napa/Sonoma, California 2019

completed, 2022

A 1,000sf residence for a chef and winemaker who believe in focussing on their craft and family. The house is off the grid on a large piece of property that straddles both Napa and Sonoma County.

project team: Brandon Jørgensen, Lisha Zhang, Dora Tam, Jonathan Solis
renderings: Claudio Campra

warped trestle

Napa, California 2020

A 2,000 square foot residence for a couple who own some of the most successful restaurants in the city of Napa, due to their genuine pursuit of the authentic. Placed on the steepest hill in town on an almost unbuildable site, this house will resemble a trestle bridge in structure and openness.

project team: Brandon Jørgensen, David Regina
model photo: Joe Fletcher

scholars retreat (resilient 005)

Saint Helena, California 2021

A 4,600sf fire rebuild for a scientist and her two daughters, one a wine maker and the other a neurologist, who love the Napa Valley and surrounding wine country. The new house is designed to be a retreat and the center for entertaining.

project team: Brandon Jørgensen, David Regina, Granite Landis, Tristan Blackmore
model photo: Joe Fletcher

filtered lanai

Waimea, Hawaii 2022

A 3,600sf residence for a family in Hawaii who love being connected to nature and using the residence as a lanai for inspiration & entertaining.

project team: Brandon Jørgensen, Granite Landis
renderings: MIR

trailside winery
Napa Valley, California 2021 –

featured,

> may 2022 hypebeast
> may 2022 designboom

A 6,000sf winery rehab situated in the center of the Napa Valley. The design incorporates the use of a scrim to identify the winery while protecting the surrounding views from neighbors.

project team: Brandon Jørgensen, David Regina
renderings: MIR

cliffhanger cabin
Alpine Meadows, California 2021 –

A 2,500sf cabin for a couple and their two children allowing a destination of respite from their busy life in the city. The design is centered around relaxation and entertaining.

project team: Brandon Jørgensen, David Regina, Tristan Blackmore, Granite Landis
renderings: MIR

ink grade winery (resilient 006)
Saint Helena, California 2020 –

A 10,000sf winery fire rebuild situated in the heart of wine country.

project team: Brandon Jørgensen, Granite Landis, David Regina, Farzad Morè, Tristan Blackmore
renderings: MIR

triporto residence (resilient 007)
Ormos Korthiou, Andros, Greece 2023

A 2,000sf (200sm) residence for a family who split their time between the busy sophistication of London and this humble and rural island on the Aegean sea and three hours from Athens.

project team: Brandon Jørgensen, Granite Landis
renderings: MIR

ORO Editions
Publishers of Architecture, Art, and Design
Gordon Goff: Publisher

www.oroeditions.com
info@oroeditions.com

Published by ORO Editions

Design Concept: Atelier Jørgensen Architects
Typography and design: Atelier Jørgensen Architects
Front Cover Photo: Atelier Jørgensen Architects
Back Cover Photo: Atelier Jørgensen Architects
ORO Project Manager: Kirby Anderson

Special thanks to: Kathryn Jørgensen, Farzad Morè, Granite Landis, Douglas Friedman, Joe Fletcher, & Stanley Saitowitz.
In Memory of Gerard 'Roddy' Creedon

Library of Congress Cataloging-in-Publication Data

10 9 8 7 6 5 4 3 2 1 First Edition

ISBN: 978-1-957183-61-9

Color Separations and Printing: ORO Group Inc.
Printed in China

ORO Editions makes a continuous effort to minimize the overall carbon foot-print of its publications. As part of this goal, ORO, in association with Global ReLeaf, arranges to plant trees to replace those used in manufacturing of the paper produced for its books. Global ReLeaf is an international campaign run by American Forests, one of the world's oldest nonprofit conservation organizations. Global ReLeaf is American Forests' education adna ction program that helps individuals, organizations, agencies, and corporations improve the local and global environment by planting and caring for trees.

Publication is made possible by Atelier Jørgensen and the Jørgensen Family.